Fusilier Cooper

Fusilier Cooper

Experiences in the 7th (Royal) Fusiliers
During the Peninsular Campaign of the
Napoleonic Wars and the American
Campaign to New Orleans

John S. Cooper

LEONAUR

Fusilier Cooper: Experiences in the 7th (Royal) Fusiliers During the Peninsular Campaign of the Napoleonic Wars and the American Campaign to New Orleans
by John S.Cooper

First published in 1869 under the title
Rough Notes of Seven Campaigns 1809-1815

Published by Leonaur Ltd

Material original to this edition and its publication
in this form copyright © 2007 Leonaur Ltd

ISBN (10 digit): 1-84677-175-7 (hardcover)
ISBN (13 digit): 978-1-84677-175-0 (hardcover)

ISBN (10 digit): 1-84677-176-5 (softcover)
ISBN (13 digit): 978-1-84677-176-7 (softcover)

http://www.leonaur.com

Contents

Preface

The Rough Notes were written for my own amusement, but never with any intention of publishing them. The scraps that I wrote during the Campaign of 1809 were lost, with my knapsack, during my illness at Villa Vicoisa, in January 1810.

My next attempt at making notes was at Portsmouth, in 1814. In this I was greatly assisted respecting dates and the names of places by having access to the Regimental Orderly Book.

After my return home in 1815, I wrote whatever I could recollect respecting the disastrous expedition to New Orleans.

The notes have little to recommend them besides their truthfulness, and as such I submit them.

J. S. C.
Carlisle
February, 1869

I Join Up

I was born December 17th, 1787, in the village of High Startforth, near Barnard Castle. My grandmother's name was Ann Wycliffe, daughter of Ambrose Wycliffe, Esq., a lineal descendant of the Wycliffe family, one of whom was John Wycliffe the great Reformer. Ambrose Wycliffe inherited several estates, but gambling and other vices reduced him and his family to poverty.

In my youth I had a great taste for reading. In particular, those books pleased me that treated of battles, sieges, etc. Hence the wars mentioned by Josephus, with the histories of the Duke of Marlborough, Prince Eugene, Charles the Twelfth, Peter the Great, etc., delighted me.

This reading was in unison with the stormy times of 1792-3. The French Revolution was producing bitter fruit. War was raging on the continent, in which Russia, Turkey, Sweden, and Austria were engaged. Holland and Belgium were uneasy, being afraid of France. At home, Radicalism was rife. Jacobite meetings were secretly held in many towns, and these were fostered by French agents.

At last war was declared against France, and little was talked about but fighting. Great rejoicings took place when the victories of Howe, Duncan, and Nelson were announced. These were rather clouded by the Irish Rebellion and the ruined harvest. The latter event caused great distress. Flour rose in price to 7s. 6d. per stone. To add to the confusion, Napoleon Buonaparte was making mighty preparations for invading our shores: but Nelson stood sadly in his way. In 1802 a short peace was patched up.

But the tyrant could not rest, nor give up the idea of invasion; of course, war broke out fiercer than before. Great indignation was excited in the British mind at the presumption of the Corsican upstart.

Volunteer corps were everywhere formed, armed, and drilled. One was raised near Barnard Castle, consisting of 600 men, by J. B. S, Morritt, Esq., of Rokeby, the friend and correspondent of Sir Walter Scott. In July 1803 I entered as a fifer, and having got a sword by my side, I made sad havoc of the tall thistles and nettles, slashing their heads off most furiously, trying to imagine them Frenchmen.

My next step was to list into the North York Militia, in June 1806. That regiment I joined at Portsmouth, and soon after we went to camp on South Sea Common. Excited by curiosity, I visited Portsea Dock Yard, in which were some of the shattered ships that had been engaged at Trafalgar. One of them, called the *Timerare,* had a breach in her side which extended the distance of three portholes. Her masts and bowsprit all gone.

December 9th, we marched to Eastbourne in Sussex. Eastbourne is about two miles from Pevensey, where William the Conqueror landed in 1066.

To fill up the line regiments for foreign service, leave was given by Government for militia men to extend their services into the regular army. August 21st—I volunteered into the 7th Royal Fusiliers, and joined the 2nd battalion of that regiment at Chelmsford, in Essex.

In November I obtained leave of absence for six weeks,

to visit home; after which I rejoined the regiment at Colchester, and there I had a fit of sickness, and the benefit of hospital diet.

In March we removed to Wheeley Barracks, and on May 9th received orders for Ireland. April 15th—We weighed, and dropped down the Thames from Tilbury Fort to Deal, during which I was very sick. Saw the dead body of a man floating. We sailed next day through the Downs, up the English Channel, and anchored at Spithead. Again weighed, and passed through the Needles, but the wind being foul, we were about twenty days in reaching Cork. Thence we marched to Clonmel in the county of Tipperary.

While in Clonmel, a young Irishman of our regiment deserted, taking with him his arms and accoutrements; but he was afterwards taken, tried by a brigade court martial, and sentenced to receive one thousand lashes. By some means he escaped from the guard-house, and was never afterwards heard of. The inhabitants in and about Clonmel are perhaps the worst in Ireland. Many of our men were fired at while on sentry. One night several ruffians attacked a farm house in the vicinity, no doubt intending to kill the farmer, whose predecessor had been ejected; but he hid himself in an out-building. One of the gang, coming to the place of his concealment, he fired, and shot the villain dead. His body was brought in a cart next morning (Sunday,) by dragoons, and hung up, bloody and dirty as he was, in front of the Town Hall. Great crowds assembled, but of course, nobody owned him.

At the same time a noted robber, named Brennan, infested Kilworth mountains, and created great alarm. The mail coach from Dublin to Cork could not run without an escort of dragoons. Nine hundred pounds were offered for his apprehension, which was shortly after effected by the Sligo Light Company, and he was hanged at Clonmel.

War was now raging with great violence in Spain, and Sir John Moore's troops having been driven out of it, a new expedition was formed to proceed to Portugal. Among others, our regiment was ordered to embark at Cork. Great was the joy of both officers and men at this.

We sailed from the Cove on the 29th of March, 1809, and after experiencing much sea-sickness, landed April 7th, on the heights of Almada, opposite Lisbon. From Almada there is a fine view of Lisbon and the broad Tagus, in which some thousands of vessels may safely anchor.

Campaign of 1809

March 11th—We were conveyed in large curiously built boats up the Tagus to Villa Franca. The scenery was beautiful; the country on both shores of this noble river being like a garden. Nothing but villas, vineyards, olive, lemon, and orange groves could be seen down to the very brink of this mighty stream. Next day we joined a splendid brigade of guards 2500 strong.

We marched to Leyria on the 15th, and were placed under the command of General Craddock; but Sir Arthur Wellesley arriving, General Craddock was sent to Gibraltar.

May 3rd—We occupied Coimbra, a city celebrated for its Roman Bridge, large Museum, University, Library, and grand Cathedral.

While we remained in Coimbra, a grand procession took place on St. John's day. Such a scene of babyism and buffoonery I never saw before nor since. A great number of bishops, priests, monks, friars, and boys were assembled in the cathedral to accompany the image of the beloved apostle along the streets, which were lined by nearly the whole population. An English regiment was allowed to head the procession. When all was ready, a swarm of priests and boys, all surpliced and bearing candles, issued from the cathedral, followed by two priests loading a richly dressed horse, which bore on its back the image of St. John. This image was gigantic, daubed with paint, clothed in a coat of mail, a brass helmet on its head, and a spear at rest in its hand. At every step the horse took its head nodded. More priests and boys followed as before. Next came the bishop, or archbishop, carrying the host under a canopy borne by six priests. Lastly came priests bearing aloft the images of the Virgin and child, followed by more priests and more images. While the procession passed, the natives kneeled, bowed, crossed, and muttered. Where the Bible is prohibited, as in Spain and Portugal, paganism and idolatry never die.

The French army under General Soult now occupied the city of Oporto, about seventy miles north of Coimbra, and it was said that they had been plundering it during three days. Wellington decided to retake the place, ordered the army to move; and although the roads between Coimbra and Oporto were very bad, yet we reached Oporto on the fourth day, and drove out the enemy.

The last day's march was really horrible, under a scorching sun and clouds of dust. The road was narrow, and little or no water all the way. We had heavy knapsacks, sore feet, and after marching between twenty and thirty miles, for a finish, we ran, to get into action, about four miles, to a town opposite Oporto, called Villa Nova; but the enemy were beaten before we arrived, and gave us the slip by a hasty retreat. The enemy, to prevent our crossing the Douro, had burnt the bridge, therefore we had to wait for boats. Having crossed the river, we marched up the steep narrow streets. The people were mad with joy; every window, balcony, and door was crowded with people crying *"Viva Ingleses! Viva Ingleses!"* waving handkerchiefs and scattering roses, etc. on the passing troops.

We were quartered in a splendid mansion in the highest part of the city. In this palatial edifice our men did justice to a grand dinner which had been prepared for the French officers. Of this I tasted not, as I feared the food was poisoned. In the streets many Frenchman were lying dead. Some artillery were left, and 700 sick in hospital.

Oporto is large, but like most Portuguese towns, its streets are very steep and narrow, sloping down to the Douro. It may be about one hundred and sixty miles from Lisbon.

After one day's rest, we pursued the enemy on the Braga road. The rain fell heavily, and the roads became very bad. Sometimes we had to wade knee deep in mud and water. We might have avoided many bad parts of the road; but the General would not allow any break in the column, so through thick and thin both officers and men had to splash.

One day, after being well wetted, we were turned like bullocks into a damp church. What followed was really ludicrous. The building was large and lofty, and I think the whole regiment was bundled into it. In a minute or two the band had possession of the altar, and the big drummer of the pulpit. All were cold, hungry, tired, and ill-humoured. Fires were wanted, and fires were made. Smash went the forms, down came the priests' stalls. The crashing of wood, the bawling and swearing of hundreds in the blinding, choking smoke that completely filled the edifice, were awful; and when darkness set in the place was a perfect pandemoneum. During the uproar, a box of large wax candles used at the altar was found. Many of these were distributed and lighted in different parts of the church, and the scene was complete and fit for Hogarth's pencil.

We reached Braga as the rearguard of the French was leaving it. Halted in the market place. Being very hungry, I tried my hand at begging, and succeeded. A grocer gave me three good loaves. Having a few *vintins*, I bought half a gallon of good wine, to which my comrade and I sat down in the main street and did justice. While feasting we were eyed by our Colonel Sir William Myers, and Captain Percy, brother to the late Bishop of Carlisle. One of them asked for a little bread. A loaf was handed.

"Have you any wine?" The canteen was given. "Have you anything to drink out of?"

"O, yes!" and a splendid gilt china cup, fit for a king, was presented.

Seating themselves on two stones at a little distance they regaled themselves freely, and returned the remainder with many thanks.

During our rest a Barbary bullock made a furious rush at one of our company, and pushed him with great violence against a house; fortunately the animal's horns were so long that its head did not crush him, and so wide that he escaped unhurt.

In the evening we continued our march long after dark, stumbling among rocks and stones; the rain still falling, and the men silent and knocked up. Several who had wax candles lighted them, and we marched by their light. Captain Percy, who commanded our company, being mounted and ahead, passed the word for me to join him. With difficulty I got to his side.

"Have you any bread?" said he.

"Yes, sir," I replied, and gave him a loaf.

When he had done eating he said, "Should you ever be in want of my help, let me know."

Captain Percy was greatly beloved by his company. As a man, he was handsome; as an officer, kind; and as a soldier, brave and adventurous.

We followed the French as far as Pinderia; but leaving all their stores, etc., and marching by a difficult route over the mountains to Orense, they entered Spain in a most wretched condition.

In this part of the country many of the peasants wear in wet weather a cloak made of straw, which turns rain.

By countermarching we arrived at Oporto again on the 22nd; but this time we were not received with *"Viva Ingleses"* as before. Leaving Oporto, we crossed the Lake of Ovar in boats, and in two days' marches reached Coimbra.

Marched June 2nd, and crossed the country to Abrantes. This town is seated on the top and side of a steep hill. Wellington saw the importance of this place and fortified it.

In crossing the country from Coimbra to Abrantes, and being quartered with three or four more in a small house, we witnessed something strange in the conduct of a woman during what she might call prayer. The custom in Portugal is, when the church bell announces sunset, the people kneel, and while counting their beads, repeat so many Paternosters, *Ave Marias*, etc. Our hostess was nursing; the bell tinkled, down she went on one knee while supporting the child on the other, and began dropping her beads, etc. But the young one did not fancy its position, and began crying. Mamma got vexed, and shouted out *"Daubus te lave!"* or "Devil take thee!" Having ventilated thus, she went on devoutly.

While sitting in another house with the master and mistress, there was a rap at the door; it was opened, and in walked a tall man with shaven crown, clad in a long grey coarse frock-like robe, a rope girdle round his waist, slipshod and bare-legged, with a capacious bag on his shoulder. After a few words with our host, and a left handed squint at us heretics, the hostess went to a chest and took out a good sized loaf, which the visitor clutched and bagged. He then shouldered his sack, gave his blessing, and walked out.

I asked the master of the house who the strange mortal was; he replied, "That is the Padre."

I asked again, "What sort of a man is he?"

17

He shrugged up one shoulder, and said, *"Elle gosto mul-eres mouto;"* that is, "He likes the women much." Sad character for a priest.

In most of the Portuguese towns and villages may be seen a low building like an English summer house. At the back of the recess there is a rude painting of what is called Purgatory, representing a large fire, and souls in great suffering in it, holding up their hands, and crying out, *"Ora pro nobis;"* that is, "Pray for us." These words are painted above. Below, there is a slit in the stone, or wooden floor, for money to pass through, in order that a priest may be paid for liberating the poor sufferers. Now, if these so-called priests possessed any sympathy, and if there be such a place, which no sane man can believe, why do they not get them out *gratis*?

The lower orders of this nation are dirty in their persons, filthy in their habits, obscene in their language, and vindictive in their tempers. Their houses are intolerably smoky, and vermin abound.

At this period the English troops made sad work in Portugal by plundering the inhabitants. No sooner was the day's march ended, than the men turned out to steal pigs, poultry, wine, etc. One evening, after halting, a wine store was broken open, and much was carried off. The owner finding this out, ran and brought an officer of the 53rd, who caught one of our company, named Brown, in the act of handing out the wine in camp kettles. Seizing Brown by the collar, the officer shouted, "Come out you rascal, and give me your name." Brown came out, gave his name Brennan, then knocking the officer down, he made his escape, and was not found out.

During our march to Abrantes a Portuguese fingered an officer's cloak. Unfortunately for him he was caught, tied up, and well flogged. Under his torture he roared out at the top of his voice for Jesus, Mary, and Joseph, But nobody came to assist the rascal.

At this time punishment in the army was generally flogging, and the number of lashes dreadful. Frequently from 200 to 500 were given; nay, sometimes more for bad crimes. In some cases half the sentence was inflicted at once, and the remainder when the culprit's back was healed. It may be imagined that the second lashing would be worse than the first.

A man of ours was flogged for breaking into a Church and stealing some silver candlesticks. By some neglect his back festered. Being in the hospital one morning, I saw the poor fellow brought in to have his back dressed. He was laid upon the floor, and a large poultice taken off the wound. Oh! what a sickening sight. The wound was perhaps eight inches by six, full of matter, in which were a number of black-headed maggots striving to hide themselves. At this scene those who looked on were horrified.

Before this I saw a poor sickly fellow, more fit for hospital than the triangles, receive 500 lashes at once. I think his crime was stealing from his comrade.

A practice, also most fearful, had been introduced of flogging by beat of drum. The manner was ten taps were beaten on a drum between each stroke. Many were lashed into insensibility, and one who was a Brunswicker into insanity. It required strong nerves to look on. Indeed, many fainted during these prolonged punishments.

In 1807, I saw two artillery men receive 400 lashes each in Colchester Barracks, during a hard frost, the snow being three or four inches deep. Their crime was attempting to rob their commanding officer.

It has frequently been stated that the Duke of Wellington was severe. In answer to this, I would say he could not be otherwise. His army was composed of the lowest orders. Many, if not the most of them, were ignorant, idle, and drunken. It is true the troops were ill supplied with provisions in the Peninsula; it is also true they plundered when an opportunity occurred. But could a general, so wise, just, and brave as Wellington was, suffer the people that he was sent to deliver from the tyrant Napoleon to be robbed with impunity? No; he could not; he did not. By the discipline he enforced, the British army became more than a match, even at great odds, to the best of Napoleon's boasted legions.

Soldiering at the present is mere child's play compared with what it was from 1800 to 1815. The military code is more in unison with humanity. Flogging is seldom heard of. The soldier's treatment is quite different. He has now both breakfast and supper. He has no bright barrels, no hair to tie or powder; in short, he is now cared for as a man. The Duke of York deserves praise for introducing Bibles into the army. That book was not carried by us.

The camp near Abrantes was formed of pine trees and branches, each hut being made capable of containing 18 or 20 men. When rain fell, it found easy entrance, to our great discomfort.

During our stay in this camp, two Irishmen of our company, whose names were Burke and Laidlow, went a short distance into a wood and fired balls or slugs through their hands, and came bleeding into camp, stating that they had been attacked by some peasants. The colonel examined their wounds, etc., and saw through the deceit. For a wonder they escaped flogging. However, though they were crippled, he ordered them to do their duties as before.

After a halt of three weeks we marched in the direction of Madrid, and crossed the Tagus at Villa Valha, by a bridge of boats. Here the Tagus is deep and rapid, being confined between two rocky hills. Next day to Sarnades, and camped in a field of newly reaped flax. Having made huts of the sheaves, we rested tolerably, but next morning some rascals set fire to the flax, and made a terrific blaze. Of course, nobody did it. Marched to Castello Branco, and crossed the frontier into Spain. Here our general made both officers and men wade through a river when there was a bridge within a hundred yards. There were, of course, sad grumbling and sulky looks. July 9th we reached Placentia under a scorching sun. Snow on the mountain tops on our left. This is a considerable town, with an old castle and aqueduct. July 20th, we were quartered in a convent near Orapesa.

Here the Spanish army, under General Cuesta, a worthless wretch, passed us to the front, boasting they would thrash the French. They numbered about 38,000, and were dressed in blue, green, and yellow. A motley crew they were. Many of them had muskets without locks, etc.

On our march to this place, one of the 3rd, or Old Buffs, was stung by a scorpion in the head, and died in consequence. Also, a man of our company, named John Barber, marched a league with a snake in his dress cap. It had crept in during the night, and hid itself under his forage cap. After passing through an immense forest of pine trees, nearly all of which were remarkably crooked, a soldier's wife was delivered of a child, after we had halted for the night. Next morning she was placed on a horse and marched with the column.

To avoid the heat, which in Spain at this time of the year is nearly tropical, we generally began to move an hour or two before daylight, when many of the men might be seen jostling and stumbling along asleep.

We were quartered at Orapesa in a convent, and the part allotted to our company was a filthy place, arched over, and close to a vault in which the dead friars were interred. One of the company, named John Clapham, wanting to cook his dinner, sought for some fuel, but finding none, as wood is very scarce in this part of Spain, Clapham entered the vault, and throwing a friar out of his coffin, he smashed it, cooked his mess, and dined like a respectable man. Whether the ejected friar felt angry at such treatment, 'tis not for me to say, certain it was that in the dead of the night a terrible uproar was made that roused the whole convent. The men started up, seized their arms, and rushed out, crying, "What's the matter?" Some said, "The French are coming," and 'twas long before the hubbub subsided. However, Mr. Clapham and the friar were blamed for the panic, guilty or not. The real cause we never found out. Now, this Clapham was a queer fellow; he generally had plenty to eat, but where he got his eatables was quite another thing. He did not tell every one.

July 22nd, we crossed a plain to Talavera-de-la-Reyna, and drove in the enemy's outposts. On the 25th we offered battle, but the French retired. Having received reinforcements, they faced about and began to skirmish with our advanced piquets, A battle now seemed at hand.

Battle of Talavera

27th/28th of July, 1809

On the 27th there was much firing in front, and the enemy strongly reinforced, came on rapidly. To receive them the Anglo-Spanish army took up position about two or three p.m. in the following order:—Nearly all the Spanish troops were posted on the right of the British; their right resting on the river Tagus, and their left touching an unfinished breastwork thrown up on our right flank. They also occupied the town of Talavera, and were snugly ensconced in hollow ways and behind walls and hedges, with a thick wood and vineyards in their front. Thus they were screened from the view of the enemy.

The right of the British line covered the unfinished breastwork above mentioned; the centre extended over a partly exposed plain and broken ground; and the left touched a rocky mountainous ridge which ran at nearly a right angle with the whole line. On the left of the centre was a hill occupied by General Hill's division and several guns. This might be considered the key of our position, as the enemy struggled hard for its possession in the battle. Along the front ran a small rivulet, dry in many places, but where there were pools, black, ugly-looking snakes were plentiful. Of this water we had to drink. I may here remark that our brigade stood on the right of the British line.

About 6 p.m. the enemy driving in our advanced picquets, debouched in large masses between the rocky heights and the vineyards in front of the English right wing. The appearance of their black columns was very imposing, and as they moved forward rapidly, we expected an immediate attack. But seeing our line steady and ready, they suddenly halted and contented themselves with cannonading till dark. Our artillery though few in number replying briskly.

After sunset our company and a company of Brunswick riflemen, called "Death and Glory Boys," were sent forward as a piquet into a vineyard, where we laid down silently among the bushes. Though the day had been hot yet the night was very cold; notwithstanding this the order was "No great coats to be put on."

At 10 p.m. the enemy made a furious attack on the hill where General Hill's division was posted, and they succeeded in gaining the summit. For some time our men and the enemy were mixed and the contest was dubious, but ultimately they were driven down and over the snake pools again with great loss. Soon after they stole through the vineyards in front, and opened a sharp fire upon us and the Spanish left, but repulse was their portion.

Finding themselves foiled they made no more attempts during the night; so ended the 27th.

The dawn of July 28th saw more than 100,000 men standing ready to slay one another. None but those who have been in similar circumstances can even guess what is felt. Just as the sun shot his first beams over the mountains on our left, *bang* went the first gun from the enemy, and *bang* was the answer from our battery on the hill. Battery after battery now opened, that on our right joining in the fray, and firing over our heads. Who the gunners were in our battery I don't know, but an unlucky shot from it killed a Brunswick rifleman by tearing out his bowels.

By and by the cannonading nearly ceased, but it was only a prelude to more serious work. The enemy were massing for attack. The death cloud was gathering blackness, and soon burst with fury. Several columns were set in motion, and directed towards different points of our line.

One of these, after threading its way among the trees and grape vines, came up directly in our front, and while deploying, called out *Espanholas,* wishing us to believe they were Spaniards. Our captain thought they were Spaniards, and ordered us not to fire. But they soon convinced us who they were by a rattling volley. We instantly retired upon our regiment, which sprung up and met the enemy on the rising ground, but our men being all raw soldiers, staggered for a moment under such a rolling fire. Our colonel Sir William Myers seeing this, sprang from his horse and snatching one of the colours, cried "Come on Fusiliers," 'Twas enough. On rushed the Fusiliers and 53rd regiment and delivered such a fire, that in a few minutes the enemy melted away, leaving 6 pieces of cannon behind, which they had not had time to discharge. The 6 pieces were immediately rendered unfit for use, as our balls were too large for their bore.

While charging the enemy, a Frenchman fell in his hurry, and was collared by a brutal serjeant of ours, who exclaimed "I'll kill a Frenchman for once," and then deliberately shot the poor fellow dead. This serjeant whose name was Oliver, was wounded in three places while ascending the hill at Albuhera, of which he died.

The enemy having failed on the right, hurled a stronger force over the open ground against the centre. Here the battle raged with great fury, and the struggle was continued on nearly the same ground, with the utmost fierceness on both sides. For a considerable time the combatants were enveloped in a mighty cloud of smoke.

This, with the thunder of artillery, the roll of musketry, and the *huzzas* of our men as they pushed back the masses of the foe, constituted one vast continuous uproar. At this time the British guards were brought up, who charged the enemy and swept them back instantly, but pursuing them too far, they suffered heavily before support came up. This was seen by Wellington, who immediately Kent forward a body of fresh men into the fray. These, in turn, charged so roughly, that the enemy retired precipitately leaving heaps of dead and wounded.

A few minutes after one of the guards came for water to one of the pools. I said "You have had warm work, how many may your brigade have lost?"

He very drily answered, "About 600 I think."

Another lull in the storm and fresh formations. "Here they come again," said many voices; so they did, but we were ready, and gave them such a warm reception that they speedily went to the right about. As in their first attack, they now left several pieces of cannon, which we secured as before. After these two attacks and smart repulses, we were not troubled with their company any more during the battle.

In the course of the day the 26th Light Dragoons who were posted on the left of the line, and out of our view, made a dashing charge at the French cavalry, but not being aware of a deep ravine between them and the enemy, they went headlong down into it, which caused great confusion. Not disheartened the unhurt men galloped up the opposite bank, and charged through the enemy's ranks, then wheeling about they gallantly cut their way back. This was not done without great loss both of men and horses.

The battle now languished, both armies were weary, notwithstanding the light troops on both sides kept up a brisk fire, on the rocky side of the mountain on the left, long after sunset. About 11 p.m. all was still. Not a voice was heard, but the cry of agony and distress from the wounded and dying. Both armies rested on the same ground they had occupied the preceding night except our brigade, which had advanced about 200 yards.

Long before daylight next morning, we were startled by drums being beaten in the enemy's lines. Of course we expected another brush, but when morning dawned no enemy was to be seen. It was ascertained that they had in their retreat crossed a branch of the Tagus and carried away 70 or 80 cars laden with their wounded. Surely the French did not fight well in this battle, when it is considered that they threw nearly the whole force of about 50,000 upon our small army of 19,000. They had been well supplied with provisions previously. We had been half starved. They had dined on the field of battle, and liquor had been served out to them before they attacked us. This was proved by what was found in the possession of the dead. On the contrary, nothing was served out to us from 2 or 3 p.m. on the 27th, until about 10 a.m. on the 29th.

The British in this engagement lost nearly 5,000, and the enemy by their own account about 9,000. The morning after the battle, the Light Brigade consisting of the 43rd, 52nd, and 95th Regiments, joined us on the bloody field, having made a forced march of 60 miles in 24 hours. We received them with loud cheers though they arrived too late.

The first work to be done, was to remove nine or ten thousand English and French wounded into Talavera; and to bury four or five thousand dead bodies. What a task for 16 or 17,000 hungry worn out men to undertake! 'Twas impossible! We had but few tools, and the ground was hard and rocky, therefore the dead were either thrown into the dry beds of winter torrents, &c, and scantily covered with earth; or, together with dead horses, gathered into heaps and burned. The smell was intolerable. As for the wounded, they perished in great numbers while lying in the blazing sun, in want of water, dressing, and shelter.

The excitement of battle being over, we all severely felt stomach complaints. I had not tasted food for 43 hours. This was not Wellington's fault, for previous to the battle much flour had been collected, and made into bread by bakers belonging the army; but during the battle, the Spaniards had broken open our stores and left very little for us. In the heat of the fight, many of these boasting Spaniards deserted, and spread the news that the English were defeated.

About 10 a.m. on the 29th, we were served with 4 ounces of bread, which was for the next 24 hours. This might make 6 or 8 decent mouthfuls.

Early in the morning of the 30th, twenty five Spanish soldiers, dressed in white and attended by several popish priests, were marched up to the front of our regiment and shot. One a young lad of 19 or 20 years of age, dropped before the party fired. But it was of no use, for after a volley at 10 paces distance had been given by about 50 men, the whole party ran forward, and firing through heads, necks, breasts, &c, completed their horrid work. The executioners having tools with them, the bodies were hidden in shallow graves in a few minutes. These unfortunates belonged to a regiment that had given way in the late battle.

We were now in a trap: the enemy we had beaten were still more than double our number and not far off in front: another army under General Soult, perhaps nearly as numerous as that before us, had come through a mountain pass in our rear, and taken possession of the large stores of bread that we had left at Placeetia.

These two French armies, probably numbered about 70,000, well supplied with provisions, &c; while ours only amounted to 17,000 in want of nearly every necessary. We were actually reduced to a starvation point, besides being encumbered by numerous wounded. Those who were seriously crippled were left at Talavera, to whom the French behaved well.

Retreat to Badajoz

August 3rd, we retraced our steps to Orapesa, accompanied by as many of our wounded comrades as could travel; the rest were left in Talavera. Next day we crossed the Tagus at Arzobispo, broke down the bridge and took up a strong position in a wood of cork and oak. No sooner was the position taken by each regiment and the arms piled, than a general attack was made upon 200 or 300 fat pigs feeding among the oaks. These were soon settled. I chased one, but Porky was to nimble for me, it ran headlong down a steep rocky bank, swam across the river we had just passed, and gave me the slip. The commissary having no bread for us, we were marched into a newly reaped field of wheat, of which each man received a sheaf instead. Laughable it was to see hundreds of soldiers bearing away their burdens, but we could make little use of the corn for want of the means of grinding it.

In this pig-chasing an accident happened to a serjeant of the Guards, while he with hundreds more was pursuing the grunters near the bridge of Arzobispo. Running at full speed after one, the point of his pike ran into the earth and stuck fast, causing the butt-end to pass through his body. 'Twas reported that he recovered, was discharged, and afterwards kept a public-house in London.

In the evening I visited the bivouac of the 43rd, in order

to hear news of my brother, who belonged that regiment, but I found he had not arrived. One of that corps made me the noble present of a real sheep's head. I hastened home to my comrade with my prize. Placing it on a stone, I looked about for a kettle in which to cook it, but while doing so, some one grabbed it. My supper was gone. We continued our march for three days in bad rocky roads, and then halted near the river Iber. This was a desolate region truly, nothing but rugged mountains on all sides. Further than this the enemy did not follow us.

Notwithstanding our weak state through want of food, we had to drag the artillery by ropes up some steep mountains, as horses could not keep on their feet. Great numbers of these animals died. Stores and cannon were buried. Men looked like skeletons. Our clothing was in rags; shirts, shoes, and stockings were worn out; and there was no bread served out for six days. All we got was a pound of bad lean beef for each day. Happy was the soldier that had a little salt.

After leaving this horrid place, we encamped at Delatoza on the steep banks of the river Rel-Monte, where we halted and had regular rations served out. Here the Dysentery raged most awfully. That we might rest at night without sliding down the steep hill-side, we cut grave like spaces. Tents during this campaign we had none, nor yet blankets.

We slept in the open air, and this was the mode: The great coat was inverted, and our legs were thrust into the sleeves; one half was put under us, und the other half above. The knapsacks formed our pillow. Thus arranged, with forage cap pulled over our ears, we bid good night to the stars, and rested as we could.

As the river ran close by the foot of the hill on which we were bivouaced, we frequently went down to it, pulled off our shirts, washed them with or without soap, knocked them well on the flat stones, and then hung them on the rocks or bushes, picked off the vermin, and when dry, put them on again.

Quitting this place, we reached Truxillo, the birthplace of Francis Pizarro, the conqueror of Peru. The family mansion yet stands in the market place. Or the 25th we marched into Merida, a large town on the Guaduana. Outside the town are the ruins of a Roman aqueduct. Inside there is a square for bull fights. Spanning the Guaduana stands a bridge of about eighty arches, paved with large stones much worn. Many of the arches are dry.

September 3rd, we encamped in the olive groves near Badajoz, and afterwards on some high ground eight or nine miles from that city. Badajoz is strongly fortified, and has a stone bridge like that at Merida, built probably by the laborious Romans.

Upon this bridge, in 1661, the Portuguese were defeated by Don John of Austria. Badajoz and Olivenza are the two frontier fortresses of Spain on the South-west.

In this camp, called Nostra Senora de Tobo, we remained till the 6th of October and recruited our strength a little. Rations were regularly served. Soap, tobacco, sugar, and many other necessaries were procurable by those who had money.

There was also plenty of snakes, scorpions, centipedes, to be had for nothing. Sleeping one night as usual under some dry branches, with two other soldiers, a scorpion having crawled up one of the men's great coat sleeves stung him severely. The poor fellow bawled loudly, jumped up, threw off his coat, and caught the venomous rascal. His arm instantly turned blue, and he was in hospital several days.

Being the colonel's orderly, and travelling to Badajoz

one morning, I felt something stirring in the fork of my trowsers. I searched, and out dropped a young centipede; going a little further, I felt the same sort of tickling; more carefully than before, I looked and found another scamp of the same size.

In the neighbourhood of our camp were perhaps 150 bee hives. How many remained after the first week of our stay I cannot tell, but complaints being made by the proprietor, several delinquents were caught and punished severely.

One night a party of our Brunswickers committed a robbery, in which one of them lost his scimitar. This being found in the morning, led to the detection of the whole concerned. Ten of them were flogged, and it was reported that one of them became insane in consequence of his punishment.

October 7th, we moved to Olivenza, a small town 15 or 16 miles from Elvas. In Olivenza our quarters were in bomb proof barracks without ventilation. Blankets and fresh straw were issued to us, which after such a fatiguing campaign as ours had been, proved very acceptable; but indulgence was against us. Half of the army fell sick of fever, and during the following winter 29 or 30 of our company died. I think our regiment lost 200 men. The prevailing disorders were fever and dysentery. What aggravated these diseases, were the cheapness of intoxicating drinks, and the drunkenness of the men.

Towards the close of November, I had an attack of dysentery; this was succeeded by fever. A large blister was put on my back and one on each instep. I think my head was also shaved, but being a long time insensible, I remember little.

Campaign of 1810

During my illness the army marched to the north of Portugal.

Soon after the march of the army to Celorico and Guarda, the sick were removed on cars to Villa Vicosa. Nothing can exceed these abominable vehicles for jolting and intolerable noise. Each rubbishly car is drawn by two bullocks, at a pace sufficiently slow and unpleasant to wear out the patience of any healthy man, even if the roads were good.

This removal and jolting I could not bear. A violent bleeding from the nose came on, and continued till I tied some small cord tightly round my little fingers; this stopped the bleeding. To make things worse it rained. I do not think that I was quite conscious of what passed on the first day's march.

Next day, which was also wet, we arrived at Villa Vicosa. Not being able to walk without support, I remained on the car till nearly night, and was then helped up the steps of a convent. The sick not being then disposed of, I was laid down on the cold flags at the stair head, and left there till removed by order of a surgeon. A relapse of fever and insensibility was the consequence. I was afterwards carried into a corridor among perhaps 200 sick and dying men. My case was really pitiable; my appetite and hearing gone;

feet and legs like ice; the three blisters on my back and feet unhealed and undressed; my shirt sticking in the wounds caused by the blisters; my knapsack and necessaries lost; and worst of all, no one to care a straw for me. One day a woman belonging our regiment passed my bed. I called her, and asked her to bring me a little tea. I had several small loaves that I could not eat, under my pillow. These I gave her, but she forgot to bring the tea, though she often went by my couch of dried fern.

Some days after, I perceived a great stir among the sick. The reason was, orders had arrived that we should be conveyed to Elvas; a city fourteen or sixteen miles distant. In this removal, we were placed in small covered waggons drawn by mules. This time we got over the road more quickly than on cars, and arrived at Elvas safely; being only once upset on the way.

Into bomb proof barracks again. No ventilation, twenty sick men in the room, of whom about eighteen died. In this place there were one door, and one chimney, but no windows. Relapse again; deaf as a post; shirt unchanged and sticking to my sore back; ears running stinking matter; a man lying close on my right hand with both his legs mortified nearly to the knees, and dying. A little sympathy would have soothed, but sympathy there was none. The orderlies (men who acted as nurses to the sick,) were brutes. In a little time my strength and appetite began to return, consequently I asked the doctor for more bread, etc. He kindly allowed me an increase of it, and a pint of wine per day. I now got rapidly better.

While sitting on my bed one day, I was gladdened by the sound of bells ringing. No one can imagine the pleasure I felt, on being again favoured with the sense of hearing. I was afraid that it had gone for ever.

Several of us were now collected and marched up the

steep streets of Elvas, to a large building capable of holding 1,700 or 1,800 men. I think there might then be more than 1,000 in it. It had previously been used as an arsenal.

Here the pavement was our bed. Some straw, once long but now short enough, was carried out and laid in the street every morning to air, and brought in at night by the nimblest. The slow footed got none. Our daily allowance was, 1lb. of biscuit, 1lb. of salt pork, and a pint of wine. I was still very weak and deaf. My property consisted of an old coat not very red; one pair of patched trowsers; a pair of what had once been called stockings; a pair of bad shoes; and the same shirt that I had on before my first sickness. I had neither knapsack, great coat, nor blanket. These were lost at Villa Vicosa as before mentioned.

Every night I buttoned up closely, and waited till some one beckoned me to take a share of his blanket and pavement couch. But deliverance came at last; an order arrived for all the convalescents who could travel, to join the army, which had marched to the other extremity of Portugal. Accordingly all the necessaries we wanted were issued to us. In the detachment were men of nearly all the regiments in the Peninsula. Truly we were a motley group.

The first day's march was only about two leagues, or eight miles; but I managed tolerably well notwithstanding my great weakness, and I thenceforward gained strength every day.

After a tedious march in which nothing particular occurred, we arrived at Guarda, the head quarters of the Fusiliers, with lighter knapsacks than when we started. Blankets, great coats, shirts, shoes, etc., had been sold on the march and turned into bread, coffee, wine, etc. Next morning the Colonel and Captain Percy inspected six of us who belonged to the Light Company, and expressed themselves glad to see us again. They were surprised at my re-appearance, as my death had been reported. The Colonel, with a list of the necessaries that were given to each of us at Elvas, proceeded to examine our knapsacks.

"Where is your blanket?" addressing the right hand man.

"Stolen, sir," was the reply.

"Where?"

"At such a place."

"How?"

"I was cook that day, sir, and while fetching water it was taken away."

"Indeed. But where is your great coat?" speaking to the second.

"Lost, sir, while in quarters."

"Very strange," said the Colonel. Speaking to the third respecting his missing shirt.

"Worn out, sir." To a fourth about his having no shoes.

"Both pairs worn out, sir."

A fifth had lost his blanket, and the sixth both blanket and great coat, etc. The Colonel smiled, but there was bitterness in it. We knew that smile. But our amiable Captain was present. At last the Colonel sarcastically said, "It astonishes me that you Light Company Men, sly and keen as you are, should have been so *unfortunate.*"

It was more astonishing that we escaped flogging. The day following, we joined our company at the village of Marmaliera, near the river Coa.

Wine being very plentiful and cheap here, our men became very drunken, and our Captain finding on inquiry that the keeper of a wine store in the village supplied the men of his company with wine whether they had money or not, sent for him, and had him tied to a tree behind our quarters, and gave him twenty-four lashes on his breech. Thus the wine seller got payment for sixty dollars worth of wine.

Three weeks after joining my company, I was seized by

fever the fourth time, and was immediately sent off to hospital at Guarda; but the place being crowded, I was placed in the dead house all night. My cousin, Robert Cooper, was also brought in sick, and died there. How long I was ill I know not, but rallying again, I was sent off with others on a bullock car to Celorica, fifteen miles distant. The road winds down the side of a steep mountain for nearly three miles, and is very dangerous, there being neither walls nor rails on the precipitous side. Over it, one of the cars rolled, and one of our company was killed.

Having reached the valley, we got on tolerably until our bullocks took it into their heads to run away. However, we were not overturned, and the animals stopped when out of breath.

After arriving at Celorico I had another severe relapse of fever. The infection was dreadful: nearly all in the room where I was were at one time insensible, bawling out the most incoherent jabber. I had my turn of that also. Although there were about twelve of us in two small rooms, there was not a single chamber utensil. A blanket was spread on the floor instead. Some made use of a window for every purpose. I saw neither basin, soap, nor towel. Such was the place, and such our condition. While at Celorico I saw one of the 27th regiment hanged for robbery. On the same tree, a short time before, three of his comrades were hanged for a similar offence.

However, having a good constitution, I soon recovered, and returned to Guarda. Guarda is said to be the highest town in Europe. Though so elevated, you can see nothing beyond its walls until about 10 a.m., when the dense fog clears off, and then the view is splendid.

The whole army was at this period quartered in the great plain which lies between Guarda, Celorica, and Almeida. Our company having removed to a village called

Musella, four or five of us were quartered in a house said to be haunted, and called by the natives *Mala Casa*. Whether this tale was true or not, this is a fact, that one night all our belts and pouches were thrown with great violence over our resting place to the floor, a distance of seven or eight feet.

Our next move was to the banks of the Coa, a few miles from the city of Cuedad Roderigo, now besieged by the French army under Marshal Massena.

While the siege was going on, Captain Percy went out daily to reconnoitre. Being often observed by the enemy, they laid in ambush and took him prisoner. Just before this, the Captain had flogged in the village a Portuguese peasant, for striking his servant with a hoe. Captain Percy was a favourite with Wellington, and much and deservedly loved by his company.

After a vigorous resistance, Cuedad Roderigo surrendered, and then the French advanced and invested Almeida. We retired into Guarda, and were quartered in a convent, from which the nuns had fled. That part of it occupied by our company had been the hospital. A skull found on the altar was used as a football, and the figures of saints arranged on one side of the room were quickly changed into dapper soldiers by being dressed in our clothes and belts, &c.

Wishing to improve my appearance, I turned tailor, and after very serious deliberation I ripped up and turned my trowsers, in order to have the better side out. In the process I made sad mistakes. Among these blunders, I ran a strong needle nearly three-quarters of an inch into my knee joint. However, by using great care I drew it out without breaking, and felt no bad effects afterwards except a little stiffness.

About this time a bloody action was fought between

our Light Division and an overwhelming body of French, near Almeida. Notwithstanding the great disparity of numbers, our gallant fellows made good their retreat across the Agueda. Both sides suffered greatly. The siege of Almeida did not last many days.

A shell from the French fell into the powder magazine which was near the ramparts, and blew it up, with some scores of houses near it. The explosion also threw down a large part of the ramparts into the ditch, thereby making a way for the enemy to enter. In consequence, the town was surrendered. Fort Conception, near Valde Mula, was also blown up.

We now began our memorable retreat to the lines of Torres Vedras. Of these formidable works we had heard vague reports, but they were not much spoken of. Massena having got possession of Almeida, moved forward with perhaps eighty thousand men into the plain in front of Guarda. Our army at this time, including the Portuguese, might number between forty or fifty thousand. All were now in motion. Hundreds mounted the ramparts to watch the advancing enemy and our retreating columns. Many eyes also were turned towards the towering beacon built on the top of Guarda's ancient castle.

During this stir several men who had broken into deserted houses were being flogged in the street with ropes, cats not being at hand. Just as the flogging was over, flames blazed from the beacon. This was the appointed signal for our evacuating the place. Our march was down a mountain side in the dark, across a valley, and up the opposite steep, by a narrow path, in which we frequently had to pull one another up.

September 4th, we halted at a place called Cea: the enemy not pressing us. After halting at Cea eleven days, we marched on the 23rd, and took up a strong position on the heights of Busacco and prepared for battle. Skirmishing began on the 25th, and continued all that day and the day following.

Battle of Busacco

September 27th/28th, 1810

On the morning of the 27th of September, 1810, 75,000 or 80,000 Frenchmen were drawn up before us within cannon range.

The position we held was higher than that of the enemy Behind our centre there was a still higher ridge, covered with trees. Near its summit, Lord Wellington took up his quarters in a spacious convent, whence he could see both armies. Our brigade was posted on the left of the whole army. The length of the English line was about two miles. The high road from Viseu to Coimbra passed through the centre of both armies.

The enemy's first attack was made against the right of our position. They mounted the steep ridge with great resolution and nearly gained the summit but a charge being made by our troops, they were driven down faster than they got up. This attack was hidden from our view by a spur of the mountain. After this failure, little more of consequence took place this day, excepting the skirmishing of light troops. When night ended the strife; fires were lighted by both armies, as the weather was cold. The appearance of these numerous watch fires was really splendid.

During a part of this night, I was placed on sentry among wet grass and bushes down a slope next the enemy. With empty stomach, and cold feet, my mind turned homeward, and I could not help wishing for "my ain fireside" and warm hearth. Such moments soldiers have.

Early on the 28th, a great stir was observed in the enemy's lines indicative of a coming storm. Presently our advanced sentries opened fire upon the enemy's light troops that came swarming out of a wood a little on our right. Immediately two heavy columns followed, directed towards the most accessible parts of our position, while our chain of piquets retired leisurely, firing into the masses of the enemy. We watched these movements with great interest. Our troops posted on the point of attack, were now drawn back a few paces behind the brow of the ridge, "Now for it! Now for it!" were the half suppressed exclamations. The enemy out of breath gains the summit. Instantly a shout, loud and protracted, rends the air, and the head of the enemy's column is annihilated by tremendous vollies. The hapless shattered mass staggers, breaks, turns, and rushes down the steep like an avalanche, while bullet, ball and shell plunge into the fugitive crowd. The enemy never stops till the wood is reached again.

In this attack the enemy's loss was heavy: General Simon who commanded the column and 500 men were taken prisoners. At the sight of the rout of the enemy, "Hurrah! hurrah!!" rose on all sides.

The other column which issued from the wood at the same time in the morning, made an attack a little further to the right, but after some hard fighting was driven down also.

While the contest was raging, sixteen or seventeen deserters, chiefly Germans, came over to us.

A little incident occurred about the same time, between the two armies. In our front stood several haystacks, to which the enemy had a fancy, but we had an objection. When we saw some French batmen sent to fetch the hay, an officer and six of us volunteered to go and burn the stacks. The enemy's foragers seeing us approach, started without their loads and gave an alarm. We had only time to fire one rick before a party of forty or fifty of the enemy prepared to pounce upon us. We therefore chose to retreat, and without loss gained our position safely.

In the course of the day Wellington and his Staff rode along the line, in view of the enemy, and were received with great cheering by each regiment as they passed.

The French General finding all his attacks fruitless, hurried off large bodies of troops round our left flank, hoping to cut off our retreat. In consequence of this movement, which we could plainly see, we denied from the blood stained ridge of Busacco before daylight on the 29th, and entered Coimbra next day; thus securing our passage across the Mondego.

The Retreat to Torres Vedras

October 1st, we crossed the river; the enemy close on our rear. In order to let the artillery and cars bearing the sick and wounded pass, we halted a few minutes under some lime trees on the road side.

While ten or twelve of us were standing under one of these, which was apparently quite sound, it suddenly broke within a few inches of the ground, and fell upon us knocking some down. Providentially, one of its large branches stuck in the earth and partly bore it up. Had this not happened, several would have been maimed or killed. This event was construed as portending some coming disaster.

Next day, a great quantity of stores was destroyed, and at Leyria one or two drunken soldiers were hung for plundering.

Distressing were the every day scenes now witnessed. Thousands, and tens of thousands of the Portuguese population crowded the narrow roads leading to Lisbon; frequently mixing with, and impeding the retreating army. These miserables, having buried their valuables, and left their homes, were staggering along carrying their children and heavy burdens. To complete the misery of all, rain fell heavily day after day; so that the roads, always bad, were by the passage of Artillery, Baggage, and Cavalry, made nearly impassable. Several men, not being able to keep up, were taken prisoners.

On the 10th, we entered the famous lines of Torres Vedras, and took up our quarters in the village of Bibaldinea, about fifteen or twenty miles from Lisbon.

Before reaching the lines, the 9th company of our 1st Battalion was attacked by a body of French, and driven down a hill. In the fray and while running, one of our men fell and was collared by a Frenchman. An Irishman, seeing the struggle, ran his bayonet through the Frenchman with such force that he could not withdraw it. Twisting it off, he left it in the poor Gaul and ran on.

On entering Sobral, the French Cavalry got orders to be ready for the saddle next morning at three o'clock. That hour passed, but no movement in advance took place, and daylight showed the wisdom of waiting, for half an hour's march would have brought them within the range of a monster battery.

Here Massena stuck for six weeks, although he had boasted that he would speedily drive the English into the sea. Instead of which he was driven to the end of his wits, how he should get out of this tremendous trap. Before him stood the combined English and Portuguese hosts, now nearly equal in number to his own, posted on rugged heights, scarped in front and flank, bristling with about 500 pieces of cannon, and extending above twenty miles, from Villa Franca on the Tagus, to the sea.

Behind these formidable lines, which were triple, floated a large fleet of our war ships, ready for any emergency. Here our rations were regularly issued, on account of our proximity to the Tagus.

Behind and around the French Marshal there was nothing but desolation. The people were nearly all gone, and their property either hidden or destroyed. Provisions for his troops could not be obtained without detaching large bodies of men to protect the coming stores; and the transport of which, if obtained, must come from Spain, a distance of 150 or 200 miles.

To harass these convoys, several hundreds of Portuguese Militia under an English Colonel (Wilson), ranged the country between the Mondego and Duero rivers. On one occasion they surprised the French garrison in Coimbro, and made them prisoners, with 5,000 sick who were in hospital; and after this they broke down one or two arches of the bridge. This was a sad blow to the enemy, for neither supplies nor reinforcements could now arrive but through the mountains.

In this manner the two armies remained without much fighting from the 10th of October until the 19th of November, 1810. In the daytime the average distance between the hostile hosts might be a mile, but at night the advanced sentries were within pistol shot.

Though we were not allowed during these wearisome six weeks to strip off either belts or clothes; yet cleanliness was insisted upon. Every regiment was also required to be on its respective parade ground an hour before daylight, in full marching order. To strengthen the already impregnable redoubts, etc., working parties were sent daily to handle the pick and shovel on the mountain tops and sides.

To the disgrace of our army, many men deserted here. Five of our regiment did so. One of the 27th regiment tried this, but he was taken, and shot.

One night a serjeant silently entered the room where twenty or thirty of us were lying on the bare ground, and in a low voice, said, "I want twenty volunteers directly." In a minute or two, he had the number. I said, "I will go, if you like." One was turned back and I went. We put our great coats over our belts and marched down to the advanced piquet. Two officers and a serjeant then went forward to the most advanced sentry, who told him that the enemy were surely aware of us, for they had doubled their sentries. We therefore returned without attempting anything further.

On another night, some sharp firing began between our piquets and the French, and all were roused instantly. What the cause was we never learned. In the hubbub the owner of a large wine store immediately let off his immense wine butts, and flooded the celler nearly mid-leg deep. This being speedily known, scores of our men ran and filled vessels of every description, and sad drunkenness ensued. Many were flogged next morning and sobered.

Now came a change. Famine had done its work. Not a Frenchman could be seen on the morning of November 19th. We moved after them to Azambuza. The enemy next made a stand at Santarem, having a river and morass in front, and the broad Tagus on their left. To further strengthen their position, they cut down hundreds of olive trees, and having sharpened the ends of the branches, placed them in rows in the manner of *cheveau de friese*. Batteries were also placed at all commanding points. Here again the sentries were within speaking distance, on a long narrow bridge. One of our first battalion was hung at this place for robbery and desertion. Our next move was to Avarias de Cema.

Campaign of 1811

While in an old house in this village, we probed, as was usual, the earthen floor with a ramrod, to ascertain whether anything was hidden, and we found a box, in which was a bag of Indian corn, etc. This was taken by one of our men who had been a miller, to a windmill at some distance. He set it agoing, and ground the corn, of which we made several messes of passable porridge. In another house, in which our band was quartered, a native entered one day, and having raised a flag, he took out of a hole a jar full of money. They had not probed well in that house.

At this place Lord Wellington reviewed our division, which consisted of three brigades, and numbering nearly 6,000. The right brigade was made up of the 27th, 97th, and 40th regiments, with a company of the 60th rifles. The centre was composed of the 11th and 23rd Portuguese regiments. The left consisted of the 23rd Welsh Fusiliers, and two battalions of the 7th, or English Fusiliers, with a company of Brunswick riflemen. A brigade of artillery, *viz.*—five guns; and a howitzer was also attached. Our brigade was called the Fusilier brigade. General Sir Lowry Cole commanded the division.

During the night of the 5th of March, 1811, the French continued their disgraceful retreat towards Spain, leaving straw sentries to deceive us Their sick were left behind. At noon we entered Santarem, and found it such a scene of filth, ruin, and desolation, as words cannot describe. Every house was gutted. Floors, furniture, and doors broken and burnt. A hot pursuit commenced next day; and although few prisoners were taken, yet many dead Frenchmen were lying on the road side. These had probably been murdered by the enraged natives. Two men and one woman were lying dead in a small village; and these sights became very common. At Pombat there was some sharp skirmishing near the old castle, and during the night the enemy set fire to a large convent, and other buildings.

Skirmish at Redinha

March 13th, 1811

Next day, the enemy being hardly pressed, made a stand near the village of Redinha. After skirmishing in a wood on our left, we debouched into the open plain, and prepared to attack. "Form close column;" "prime and load;" "fix bayonets;" "shoulder;" "slope;" "silence;" "steady;" "deploy into line;" "forward." We moved across the plain in three or four parallel lines towards the French batteries, which now opened upon us briskly. This was immediately followed by as heavy a fire of musketry as I ever heard in the Peninsula. The balls flew from both combatants like hail. But this duel did not last long: the enemy gave way, and carried off their artillery at a rattling pace, followed by loud English hurrahs, and our skirmishers. We hurried through the burning village to overtake them; but they waded the river, and made good use of their legs. Marshall Ney commanded the retreat, and did it well, so that few prisoners were taken.

In this rough skirmish I noticed a German woman belonging the Brunswick rifles, trudging boldly close behind her husband, with a heavy load on her back, in the midst of the fire.

In the morning the French set the beautiful little town of Condexia on fire, which, together with the Queen's palace that stood in its midst, they left in names. This was the general proceeding of the French during their retreat. Whenever we gained any high ground, the track of their march might be discovered by smoking towns and villages.

After passing through Condexia, the enemy being pressed by our light division, took to the mountains; as the bridge at Coimbra was partly broken down, and guarded by Colonel Wilson and some Portuguese militia, consequently their plans were deranged, and their privations multiplied.

Next day there was much firing and hurried marching. We encamped at night near the village of Espenhel. Had nothing to eat but boiled bean tops. I could not relish them. The officers were just as badly off as ourselves. The cause was we had outmarched our stores.

The following day an order arrived for our division to counter-march and join General Hill, as another French army had broken into Portugal on its eastern side. Off we started and made a forced march on the 16th over hilly stony roads without a mouthful of bread. Great numbers of men unable to keep up; remained on the road or in the fields during a wet night. As for myself, I hobbled on with the column; but I suffered dreadfully from hunger, thirst, little shoes, and blistered feet.

Skirmish at Campo Mayor

March 25th, 1811

After a day's halt we continued our march to Campo Mayor, a small fortified town which the French had breached and taken a few days previously. Having marched rapidly, we surprised the garrison so completely that they had to use both the main gate and the breach in their hurry to leave the place.

Had they not had many cavalry, we should have made them all prisoners in their retreat across the plain to Badajoz. As it was, they lost nearly 700 killed and wounded. We also took several pieces of cannon, but owing to the small force that had got up, the enemy rallied and carried them off.

We gave up the pursuit a few miles from the town, but our cavalry followed till checked by the guns of Fort Christoval, a distance of perhaps fourteen miles.

During this running fight, an encounter took place between a French colonel of heavy cavalry and a corporal of our 16th Light Dragoons. The corporal had killed a French cuirassier in the view of this officer. Being enraged, the colonel attacked the English horseman and wounded him slightly. The corporal being a good swordsman and not much disabled, by a skilful stroke cut the fastening of the colonel's brass helmet, which falling off, he followed up his blow with a terrible backhanded sweep of his sword, and struck off the upper part of the colonel's skull close to his ears. I viewed his body a few minutes after his death. His brains had fallen out and the cavity was empty. An officer with a flag of truce came next day to search for his body; of course leave for this was granted and he was taken away. I heard afterwards that the colonel was a French Marquis.

April 1st, we moved to Elvas, a strong place within sight of Badajoz. This city is supplied with excellent water by a splendid aqueduct, having five tiers of arches. On the opposite side of the city about 1,000 yards distant, stands a strong fort on a high conical hill which might be made impregnable. Our next move was to Zeruminha, where we constructed a bridge on large barrels, etc., across the Guaduana. In the vicinity a troop of our 13th Light Dragoons was surprised and many of them taken prisoners. On the 8th, we invested the town of Olivenza, which not being strongly garrisoned surrendered on the 15th.

Here a fit of ill humour cost one of our company his life. His name was David Wilson a handsome young Irishman. For some fault, a lieutenant ordered him an extra tour of duty. Accordingly, when the time came for relieving a small firing party that was placed under the wall to draw off some of the fire from our battery, he was sent along with others to that post. In that dangerous place it was necessary to keep close under cover, instead of which, David stood bolt upright before the enemy, and was directly shot right through the heart. An officer, asked, "Who will volunteer to fetch the body?" Four of us volunteered, but we found it no easy task, as the place was quite exposed to the enemy's fire. At last we made a dash, threw the body into a great coat, and ran down an open sewer full of filth. A shower of balls came whizzing, but no harm was done, except a man's neck being grazed by a ball.

After the town had surrendered, we marched to Merida

where we suffered much, as the rations were insufficient. Many a meal we made of fried bullock's blood; and that man was counted happy who possessed a little salt. When a bullock was killed there was a grand scramble for the blood. A bullock's tail was sold for sixpence or a shilling; its liver for five shillings, and a biscuit weighing three quarters of a pound would bring five shillings also.

On the 7th of April, we opened trenches for the first time before Badajoz. On the 14th the enemy made a sortie but were driven back in a hurry.

One day during this short unsuccessful siege, while our company was in the trenches waiting for the engineer to stake out some more work, a party sat down to play cards in the trench. My duty was to warn the men of coming shot or shell. A burst of smoke: I bawled out: "Take care." *Whew, whew, whew:* all were silent. The shell strikes the ground, rebounds, rolls up the outside of the parapet, and falls over the shoulder of a card player, whose name was Arundel, into the trench between his legs. A scramble ensued. After a pause a soldier seized the shell and threw it out of the trench. When examined, 'twas found that by some means the fuze had been destroyed.

Battle of Albuhera

May 16th, 1811

To prevent us taking this fortress, a large army under
General Soult was assembled, and marched to relieve it.
Therefore General Sir William Beresford sent off the guns,
stores, etc., to Elvas, and prepared to meet the enemy near
the village of Albuhera. Of the enemy's approach we had
no idea or apprisal. But about midnight on the 15th, we
were suddenly ordered to march, weary and jaded as we
were with being on piquet duty near the city walls for
thirty-six hours.

After marching till daylight appeared, we halted and put
off our great coats. Every one was complaining of want
of rest and sleep. Having marched a few miles further up
a valley we heard distant sounds, and though they grew
more frequent, yet we did not think that they were the
noises of a battle field, as we were quite ignorant of any enemy being near. But so they proved, for in a few minutes
the words, "Light Infantry to front," "trail arms," "double
quick," were given. We then knew what was astir. Being
tired, we made a poor run up a steep hill in front; but on
reaching its summit we saw the two armies engaged below, on a plain about three quarters of a mile distant.

The French army consisted of 22,000 infantry and 4,000
cavalry. Our army was composed of about 7,000 English,
2,000 Portuguese, and 16,000 Spaniards; but on these we

did not place any confidence. Of cavalry we had perhaps 1,200 or 1,400. I do not know the number of our guns, but I do remember that the French had more than double the number of ours.

We were now quite awake and roused in earnest. Towards the centre of the line we moved rapidly; then formed close column, and lay down in a storm of hail and rain waiting for orders.

During the blinding shower of hail, etc., the French, having crossed the river which ran between the two armies, made a furious onset on the Spanish right wing which was posted on a hill, and drove it in great confusion into a hollow.

In moving to the right, to regain the ground thus lost by the Spaniards, General Hill's right brigade suffered dreadfully. The carnage was awful on both sides, and the dead lay in rows where they had stood. What greatly contributed to the slaughter of our men, was an attack made by a body of Polish lancers on Hill's right, before it got solidly formed. The day was now apparently lost, for large masses of the enemy had gained the highest part of the battle field, and were compactly ranged in three heavy columns, with numerous cavalry and artillery ready to roll up our whole line. The aspect of that hill covered with troops directly on our flank was no jest, as we had no reserve to bring up.

At this crisis, the words, "Fall in Fusiliers," roused us; and we formed line. Six nine pounders, supported by two or three squadrons of the 4th Dragoons, took the right. The 11th and 23rd Portuguese regiments, supported by three light companies, occupied the centre. The Fusilier brigade with some small detachments of the brigade left at Badajoz, stood on the left. Just in front of the centre were some squadrons of Spanish cavalry. The line in this order approached at quick step the steep position of the enemy; under a storm of shot, shell, and grape, which came crashing through our ranks.

At the same time the French cavalry made a charge at the Spanish horse in our front. Immediately a volley from us was poured into the mixed mass of French and Spaniards. This checked the French; but the Spanish heroes galloped round our left flank and we saw them no more.

Having arrived at the foot of the hill, we began to climb its slope with panting breath, while the roll and thunder of furious battle increased. Under the tremendous fire of the enemy our thin line staggers, men are knocked about like skittles; but not a step backward is taken. Here our Colonel and all the field-officers of the brigade fell killed or wounded, but no confusion ensued. The orders were, "Close up;" "Close in;" "fire away;" "forward." This is done. We are close to the enemy's columns; they break and rush down the other side of the hill in the greatest mob-like confusion.

In a minute or two, our nine pounders and light infantry gain the summit, and join in sending a shower of iron and lead into the broken mass. We followed down the slope firing and huzzaing, till recalled by the bugle. The enemy passed over the river in great disorder, and attacked us no more, but cannonading and skirmishing in the centre continued till night.

Thus ended the bloody struggle at Albuhera, 16th of May, 1811. The enemy ought not to have been beaten, for they were greatly superior in all arms, besides having an advantageous position. To allow a line two deep without reserve, with few guns and cavalry, to drive them from a hill was positively shameful. Had those columns been deployed into line and properly led, they might have swept us from the hill side like chaff. But they did not.

Having returned to the top of the ridge we piled arms and looked about. What a scene! The dead and wounded lying all around. In some places the dead were in heaps. One of these was nearly three feet high, but I did not count the number in it.

When our regiment was mustered after the battle it numbered about eighty. As we went into fire 435 strong, we lost 355. The first battalion some hundreds stronger than ours lost 353. All the three colonels of our brigade fell on that hill side; *viz*: Colonel Sir William Myers, killed; Colonels Edward Blakeney and Ellis, wounded.

What was now to be done with the wounded that were so thickly strewed on every side? The town of Albuhera had been totally unroofed and unfloored for firewood by the enemy, and there was no other town within several miles; besides the rain was pouring down, and the poor sufferers were as numerous as the unhurt. To be short, the wounded that could not walk were carried in blankets to the bottom of the bloody hill and laid among the wet grass. Whether they had any orderlies to wait on them, or how many lived or died, I can't tell.

But if they were ill off our case was not enviable. We were wet, weary and dirty; without food or shelter. Respecting the wounded, General Blake, the Spanish Commander, was asked to help us with them, but he refused to send any men to carry them off.

We lay down at night among the mire and dead men. I selected a tuft of rushes and coiled myself up like a dog, but sleep I could not, on account of hunger and cold. Once I looked up out of my wet blanket, and saw a poor wounded man stark naked, crawling about I suppose for shelter. Who had stripped him or whether he lived till morning I know not.

Before daylight we were under arms shivering with

cold, and our teeth very unsteady; but the sun rose and began to warm us. Half a mile distant were the French, but neither they nor we showed any desire of renewing hostilities. A little rum was now served out, and our blood began to circulate a little quicker. We then rubbed up our arms and prepared for another brush; but nothing serious took place, except cavalry skirmishes on the plain before us. Towards evening the enemy retreated into a wood two miles off, and next day disappeared.

In this action the English and Portuguese lost between 4,000 and 5,000 in killed, wounded, and missing. The Spaniards suffered little. The enemy's loss was very great. Wellington arrived from the north of Portugal a few hours after the battle. Had he come sooner we should have had more confidence of victory. This may appear from the brief dialogue which took place between one Horsefall and myself, when marching to attack the dark columns on the hill.

Turning to me Horsefall dryly said, "Whore's ar *Arthur?*" meaning Wellington.

I said, "I don't know, I don't see him."

He rejoined, "Aw wish he wor here."

So did I.

On the 19th, we left this bloody field, and encamped in the wood which the French had left. Here all the water we used, had to be fetched two miles. Our next move was to Almanderlaho.

But mischief was again brewing. The French being de-termined to relieve Badajoz advanced in great force, per-haps 70,000, therefore we retired, crossed the Guaduana and encamped close to the gates of Elvas; but some mis-take kept us out all night, in a terrible storm of thunder, lightning, and rain. A thunderbolt fell near us, shivering one side of a tree from top to bottom, and killing some mules. In the morning, the authorities let us into the town. Thence we marched and encamped at Toro de Moro near Campo Mayo. The French were in Badajoz, which was only a few miles distant, but though they were double our numbers they never made an attack; perhaps remembering Albuhera and the 16th of May, 1811.

At this camp the army that had been fighting at Sabugal and Fuente-de-Honore, in the north of Portugal, joined us. Both they and we had had some severe work since we parted at Espenhel on the 16th of March.

Orders were here received that our skeleton regiment should be incorporated with the 1st Battalion; with these exceptions, that the officers, non-commissioned officers, and band, should go to England. Being only lance corporal, I had the mortification of being transferred, and of seeing my old comrades march merrily from the camp for old England.

Scorpions, lizards, and other vermin where plentiful here among our huts. Turning up a flat stone that I wanted one day, I found a large scorpion embedded under it. Having read that a scorpion would kill itself when irritated. I poked it out of its bed and encircled it with red hot embers. It ran round a few times, but finding no way of escape, it lashed both its sides most furiously with its sting -armed tail which emitted a dark fluid at every stroke. In a minute the animal was dead.

July 21st, we commenced a long march to the north of Portugal and arrived at Fuente Grinaldo, on the 24th of September. It was here reported that during our march, on the 1st of August, the day being excessively hot, and water scarce, that six men died on the road.

The stores not having arrived, we were ordered to dig potatoes in the fields, of which we had two pounds served out to each man, instead of one pound of biscuit. This was a poor exchange, for the potatoes were like lead. Our next move was to Aldea-de-Bispo, where I attained full corporalship. We were now a few miles from Cuedad Roderigo, which place had been blockaded by a part of our army about a fortnight.

To drive us away, the French collected a large force, and furiously attacked our 3rd division; but, General Sir Thomas Picton, who commanded it, seeing no chance of maintaining his post, retreated. Being hardly pressed, by overwhelming numbers he formed the division into squares, and kept the enemy at bay. In this predicament, repelling every charge, he retired several miles over very rough ground without great loss. When the cannonade became serious, our brigade was ordered to advance with all haste to assist the retiring division. The sight of our men in squares, marching as steadily as in a field day, was splendid. When within 300 yards of the enemy, we halted, and formed square. The French halted also, while our artillery made sad gaps in their ranks.

Having stood in this manner two or three minutes, a French officer, perhaps a General, came cantering to within fifty or sixty yards of our front, and having satisfied his curiosity or impudence, he fired his pistol at our general and galloped off like an Arab. "Brunswick, give him a shot;" cried the general, to a Serjeant of the Brunswick Rifles. The serjeant ran forward eight or ten paces, kneeled and fired, but missed his lordship.

An officer now hastily approached our general, and informed him, that he had just arrived from England and brought 400 men, mostly recruits, for our regiment. He asked if they might be brought forward, "No, no," said the general, "Take them away; take them away."

As the French were now concentrating in vast numbers, we retired slowly to some earthworks on a small eminence, while the enemy poured into the plain before us by thousands, and took up a position half a mile in front of us. This affair happened near the village of El Bodon.

A strict watch was kept all night, but the enemy made no forward movements. Next morning, Lord Wellington came to a small battery which had been constructed in front of our bivouac, and laying his glass on the top of a gun, viewed the enemy's lines from right to left. One of his Aides asked him what number of French were before us, he gravely replied, "I think there are about 60,000." I confess, I was uneasy; for I could see no more than 5,000 or 6,000 of our troops. Without molestation we remained in our position till a little after dark, and then retired in silence, leaving piquets to mask our retreat. We marched all night in a heavy fog which nearly blinded us, and in the morning halted near Fuente Grinaldo.

Skirmish at Aldea-De-Ponte

September 27th, 1811

Scarcely had we got our stinking messes of meat half boiled, when an order was given to fall in immediately. I was ordered to take a file of men and follow the Brigade Major to the front. Over some stone walls we climbed into a wood of cork trees; leaving marks to guide us back to the regiment. Halting in a shady spot the Major went forward to watch the advancing enemy. We followed him a little to have a peep, and from a cover of brush wood saw our horsemen skirmishing and retiring slowly from rock to rock, before a large force of the enemy's cavalry.

Unlooked for, and unperceived by us, a body of French infantry was stealing rapidly up a valley 200 or 300 yards distant. The Major returned, and ordered us to retire quickly. We rejoined our company just as the enemy's skirmishers opened fire upon us. Here two of us made our wills.

My comrade said, "If I be killed, you take my knapsack."

I said, "If I be killed, you take mine."

In a minute or two after the action began, my comrade the will maker was wounded in the belly and hand; I never saw him afterward.

We then rushed over a hedge into a pelting fire, at the same time our Colonel, (General Sir Edward Packenham,) galloped into the melee with his cocked hat under his arm, shouting "Forward, Fusileers!" We dashed forward indeed, and the enemy were driven in confusion into the valley whence they had issued. Our men pursued them more than a mile, but about sunset, a body of them dressed in their great grey coats were perceived among the trees and bushes stealing upon us. There being not more than fifty of us together, we fell back until a wing of our regiment came up, and then a smart fire was thrown into their ranks, and kept up in a wood till after dark. In this action I was nearly made prisoner by three Frenchmen. In this rough skirmish a cannon ball struck a heap of stones, one of which gave me a blow on the right shoulder; however, it did no injury, as I wore what are called wings on my jacket. Having repulsed the enemy, we encamped on a hill side near where we fought. The night was cold, and what was worse, eatables were short. Marched again at midnight, and stumbled on in bad roads till daybreak.

November 4th, we were quartered in Campillo, where hunger drove us to seek and eat roasted acorns.

On the 29th, we waded over a frozen rivulet to Villa de Cubo, a miserable village.

Campaign of 1812

January 8th, we crossed the Agueda at Celices-el-Checo, and commenced the Siege of Cuedad Roderigo. The Divisions ordered on this service were the 3rd (Picton's), 4th. (Cole's), and the Light Division (Crauford's). Each division in turn sent strong detachments to open and guard the trenches, etc.

A strong redoubt or fort which prevented approach, to the wall was stormed by the Light Division with, little loss. Ground was then broken; but we did not fancy either pick or shovel, for men cannot make much progress with one meal in twenty-four hours.

On the 15th, I volunteered out of my turn for the trenches, and fell in about three a.m. 'Twas bitterly cold, and there was no breakfast in those days. The adjutant called me out of the ranks and ordered me to take a party of batmen and mules, and carry pine logs to the bivouac before Roderigo. But where were the logs? They were growing in a neighbouring wood. It was a pretty job I had with, six lazy batmen, six stupid kicking mules, and only two or three blunt tomahawks.

At last we got loaded and under way, but the loads were never content to ride decently: they were continually forming triangles or gravitating to earth. After much vexation I got to camp, and found the officers sitting in shallow pits round burning logs; but the men had neither shelter nor fires.

At this moment a relief for the trenches was falling in. "Corporal —— where are you?"

No answer. I snatched up my piece and marched off in corporal somebody's room to fill sand bags, etc., for a nearly completed battery. An engineer gets on the top of the battery to superintend the laying of the bags, a shot comes and cuts him in two. His dollars fly about. At this time the French, were firing most furiously to destroy the battery. While thus employed one of our officers became very ill, I helped him out of the trenches and down to camp. I then lay down on the side of a gutter and fell asleep. At daylight I awoke stiff with cold.

Being on piquet a night or two after, the enemy fired 200 shot and shell between ten and eleven o'clock. Our batteries opened next day and breaches were speedily made in the town wall.

It was our turn for the trenches on the 19th, and we fully expected to be the stormers at night, but Lord Wellington knew better than send weary men to such risky work. We were, therefore, relieved by the Light Division, and returned to our quarters five or six miles distant.

No sooner was I at home, than the adjutant favoured me with a walk back in search of a silly fellow, who had purposely shot himself through the leg or foot.

I reached the camp again in two hours, but found not the self mutilated soldier. Hearing that my brother George, who belonged to the 43rd, was in the trenches, I sought and found him under fire in the advanced sap, where men were filling and setting up gabions. Though balls were whizzing very unpleasantly about their ears, some were amusing themselves by throwing clods of earth at each other.

For a few minutes my brother obtained leave to speak with me. While chatting in the trench a round shot whizzed close past my head. We parted, he to the sap, and I to sup if possible, being hungry and tired. I found the old damp church and the straw in a corner very comfortable.

When ten o'clock p.m. arrived, we had no need of newspapers to inform us of what was going on. The rattling of musketry, the booming of cannon, and the explosion of mines, plainly told that the Light Division was storming the city. The consequences were, the place was ours and the troops that were concentrating for its relief, found that Wellington was too sharp for the best of them.

In this place were found seventeen of our men who had deserted some time before. All these foolish fellows were tried and shot in the presence of their respective divisions. Two of them belonged to our brigade.

We were marched to see the execution, on a plain near Villa de Cubo, and formed three sides of a square, the remaining side being open.

When all was ready the prisoners were drawn to the grave side on a car. One of them was elderly, the other a boy of perhaps nineteen. They kneeled on the new mould facing the guard, and were blindfolded. All were silent. An officer approaches the prisoners and reads the sentence, and then withdraws. A pause. The provost martial looks toward the General for the signal. 'Tis given. Twelve men fire. Both culprits fall forward. The boy is dead; the elder rolls in agony. More shots are fired through his head and breast, and the deserters are no more. Being laid side by side in the grave, we marched close past it in file; took a look at the bloody remains, and marched away to quarters.

Having secured the French prisoners, and filled up the trenches, we commenced our march back to Badajoz, and invested it on the 16th of March. Wellington's distribution of the army was as follows: the Third, Fourth, and Light Divisions were to besiege the town; the First, Second, Sixth, and Seventh Divisions were sent in advance to the forest of Albuhera, as a covering army; and the Fifth Division had the rough work of attacking Fort Christoval, which stands on the opposite bank of the river Guaduana.

Siege of Badajoz

March 16th-April 6th, 1812

The trenches were opened next morning (Saint Patrick's day), and the work went on with great rapidity, although rain fell in abundance many days together. The men marched to the trenches through mud; and they worked nearly mid-leg deep in mud; and to make all more miserable, they had to sleep in a muddy camp. At daybreak on the 25th, the enemy made a sortie, and rushed into the trenches; but they were as sharply driven out again. However, they carried off several shovels, etc., without asking leave.

After dark one evening, detachments from the different divisions stormed a small fort called La Picurena, which flanked our approaches. The contest was sharp but short. Bells were rung, drums were beaten, but in spite of ditch, pallisades, and garrison, our brave men gained the fort in a few minutes. A battery was formed near it, but it was too distant to make much impression on the town wall.

Another battery of twenty-four pounders was then opened at 150 yards distance, and this did its work in grand style. Salvoes brought down the wall splendidly, so that two breaches were soon made. On the 5th of April, there was a whisper abroad that the town would be stormed after sunset, but no order came.

At nine p.m. on the 6th the orders were, "Pile knapsacks by companies," "fall in, and move off silently." The night was dark, the town was still, while our batteries kept thundering away at the breach.

When our men had approached within 300 yards of the ditch, up went a fire ball. This showed the crowded state of the ramparts, and the bright arms of our approaching columns. Those men who carried grass bags to fill up the ditch, and ladders for escalading the walls, were now hurried forward. Instantly the whole rampart was in a blaze; mortars, cannon, and muskets, roared and rattled unceasingly. Mines ever and anon blew up with horrid noise. To add to this horrible din, there were the sounding of bugles, the rattling of drums, and the shouting of the combatants. Through a tremendous fire our men rushed to the top of the glacis, down the ladders, and up the breach. But entrance was impossible, for across the horrid gap the enemy had placed, in spite of our fire, a strong beam full of sword blades, etc., forming a *cheveaux de frise,* behind which, intrenched, stood many ranks of soldiers, whose fire swept the breach from end to end. Besides, the top of the parapet was covered with shells, stones, sand bags, and logs of wood, etc., ready to be thrown into the ditch. As the breaches could not be forced, and as our men kept pouring down the ladders, the whole ditch was soon filled with a dense mass which could neither advance nor retreat. Upon these the enemy threw the missiles from the parapet, with a continuous fire of musketry and round shot. My comrade was killed while descending a ladder. Some men went further to the right, and jumped into that part of the ditch that was filled with water, and were drowned.

While this murderous strife was going on in the ditch, two false attacks were made on the flanks of the city, and both these succeeded. Nearly at the same time the 3rd Division scaled the castle and got into the rear of the breaches. The enemy seeing this, retreated through the town and across the bridge into Fort Christoval. The garrison, numbering about 4,000, surrendered next morning, laid down their arms outside the walls, and were marched off prisoners.

As soon as the French had left the breach, the beam was removed, and our maddened fellows rushed into the town by thousands. Wine stores were broken open, and horrible scenes commenced. All order ceased. Plunder was the order of the night. Some got loaded with plate, etc.; then beastly drunk; and lastly, were robbed by others. This lasted until the second day after.

Next morning the numerous wounded were collected. The churches were so crowded that many were sent to Elvas. I was sent with several French wounded to a church in the city. This edifice was filled—nay, crammed with groaning and dying men. The same day, I was made serjeant. Death had made room enough: for our regiment had lost 230 officers and men, killed and wounded. As the siege had only lasted twenty days, the French were too late, as at Roderigo.

During this third siege, one of our company, named John Fletcher, a wicked, brawling fellow, lost his life in the trenches in a peculiarly awful way. Being irritated during the wet weather by almost incessant fatigue, he wished, with a dreadful oath, that when he again entered the trenches his head might be knocked off his shoulders. His head was actually blown off next day in the trenches. At the same time, a tall serjeant of ours was struck by a cannon shot in the breast and doubled up.

April 13th. We left Badajoz, and reached Aronches, where, becoming ill, I was left behind charged with the care of six sick men, and ordered to bring them on to Portalegre. How was that to be done? They were sitting on the road unable to walk. Much baggage was passing; but not one of the Spanish muleteers would take up my poor feverish men. I grew desperate. An empty car came up; I ordered my men to get into it, but the driver would not stop. I threw their knapsacks into the car; he threw them out again. Enraged, I drew my bayonet, took it by the small end, and swinging round, gave him such a blow on the mouth with the heavy end as stunned him. Then I got them on the car, and he drove on, holding his mouth as if he had got the tic. Afterwards, having got a mule or two, I got them all safely to Portalegre. From this place I was sent to hospital in a town called Aldea-de-Choa, where I remained a month. Having recovered, I took charge of the convalescents belonging to the 4th Division, and for a short time acted as serjeant-major of that depot, in which were about 600 men. While I remained here, the English army gained a great victory at Salamanca, and then marched to Madrid. But the enemy gathering in great force from all quarters, Wellington retired into cantonments near Cuedad Roderigo.

About Christmas, 1812, I was ordered to join my regiment, then lying at St. Joa-de-Piscara, on the river Douro. The party selected to march with me consisted of a sutler (a man who sells provisions, etc., in camp), his wife and servant, a private, and myself. Our first stage was Abrantes, and the road to it lay through a vast forest, perhaps twenty miles in length. This wood had a bad name, as an officer's servant had, just before our starting, been robbed and murdered in it by banditti. We set off rather late in the day, mounted on mules, and on entering the wood, loaded our pieces heavily with balls and slugs. As much rain had previously fallen, the small brooks had become like rivers. After crossing several of these, we came, a little after sunset, to one so deep and rapid that we halted to consider what we should do. Having a tall mule, I tried to ford the stream; but finding the animal about to swim, I turned back. So we lighted a fire on the bank, and prepared to camp for the night. It was frosty, and the wind cold. However, we got some supper, and sipped a little grog. Bayonets were fixed, and our arms placed against a tree within reach as we sat round the fire. Presently the party began to dose; but sleep I could not, as I had charge of the party, and knew that the sutler had a large sum of money with him. Near midnight I was startled by a loud whistle on the opposite side of the stream. I roused the party, and soon after we heard the tramp of a horse among the stones on the opposite bank. The rider halted a minute at the edge of the water, whence he could see our fire. Knowing the place, he dashed into the flood, and was beside us in an instant. He asked for a light to his cigar, and began smoking, at the same time surveying us closely. Another whistle. I looked at our arms. Again a splash into the stream, and up cantered another cloaked horseman. I listened.

"What are these?" said the last arrived, in Portuguese.

"Don't know," was the response. There was silence.

"Have they arms?" enquired the last comer. A significant silence followed, or perhaps a nod at our gleaming bayonets and knitting brows.

"Where are you going?" said I.

"Aldea-de-Choa," was answered.

"You are very late," I rejoined.

"*Ne imported,*" said one of them.

After a few more curt questions, etc., they dashed into the wood and disappeared.

In Abrantes, we found a regiment of Portuguese cavalry doing duty as infantry, by Wellington's order, for an act of cowardice.

After halting two days at Abrantes, a party, consisting of one officer, a Serjeant, and myself, with twenty-five rank and file, marched to join our respective regiments. Early one morning we found a private of the 83rd regiment dead on the road. Turning him over we saw he had been shot in the belly, and from the quantity of blood scattered along the road on a thin cover of snow, we judged he had received his death wound while attempting to rob. We left him lying. In twelve or fourteen days I joined my regiment at St. Joa-de-Pisquera. Here we wintered.

Several fresh regiments now arrived from England; among the rest, some troops of the Life Guards and Horse Guards Blue, with tents and blankets for all the army. Every man's kit was now completed. The government should also have sent us new backbones to bear the extra weight. The following is a list of articles carried by each man during the next march.

1 Fusee and Bayonet	14 lbs
1 Pouch and sixty rounds of ball, etc.	6
1 Canteen and Belt	1
1 Mess Tin	1
1 Knapsack Frame and Belts	3
1 Blanket	4
1 Great Coat	4
1 Dress Coat	3
1 White Jacket	0½
2 Shirts and 3 Breasts	2½
2 Pairs Shoes	3
1 Pair Trowsers	2
1 Pair Gaiters	0¼
2 Pairs Stockings	1
4 Brushes, Button Stick, Comb	3
2 Cross Belts	1

Pen, Ink, and Paper	0¼
Pipe Clay, Chalk, etc.	1
2 Tent Pegs	0½
Weight of Kit without Provisions	**53 lbs**
Extra Weight for Marching—	
Three days' Bread	3
Two days' Beef	2
Water in our canteens	3
	61 lbs

Besides this weight, the orderly Serjeant of each company had to carry the orderly book, whose weight was perhaps two pounds; and in turn the regimental colours.

Campaign of 1813

Having received all our stores, we crossed the Coa on the 18th of May, and the Esla on the 31st, by a pontoon bridge, where we took some prisoners. Continuing our march, we reached Palentia on the 7th of June. Palentia is on the river Carrion, and in the province of Leon, forty or fifty miles from Burgos. Leon is a beautiful and plentiful country. The French had left Palentia some hours before we entered; of course we were hailed as deliverers. On the 15th we descended the romantic slope of the Ebro. The road down to the river is exceedingly steep, paved with large stones, and was probably the work of the Romans. Plenty of cherries grew in the hedges. We encamped, sadly tired, after passing the river. Nothing could be bought here, and no rations were served out till after dark. On the 18th we reached Villa-de-Monte, and skirmished with the enemy. On the 19th the French took up a position near Moutabeta. Striking off the road to the right, we prepared for action, while the enemy's balls flew thickly among us; but seeing us press on, they retired hastily, leaving their dinners. I got nothing: the stragglers get these things. After pursuing them two or three miles, we camped.

While passing through a wood, several bags of meal were discovered, and brought to camp by our batmen, and divided among us. Glad we were of such a prize. I tried

dumpling making but the stuff would not stick together. However, into the camp kettle it went in large lumps.
When boiled, the dumplings looked like little frightened
hedgehogs. To get a mouthful, I had to pick lots of prick-
les from the mass. The material turned out to be barley
meal unsifted, and was meant for the French cavalry. Here
one of our poor fellows named Hodgson, died as soon as
he was helped from the sick car. He had been long ill of
dysentery, but would never give up marching with us till
death claimed him. A shallow grave was dug after dark in
rocky ground, and under a scanty covering of mould we
left poor Hodgson. Next day we halted, having the whole
French army, 60,000 strong, in front, commanded by King
Joseph Buonaparte.

Battle of Vittoria

June 21st, 1813

The 21st of June saw 120,000 healthy men rise from their cold beds, and prepare to slaughter one another. The morning was splendid, and all was still. A cup of coffee would have been a treat. A little before noon the order to move forward came, and in a few minutes the high road to the city of Vittoria was filled by converging masses of artillery, cavalry, and infantry, moving towards the French centre. The enemy's position was well chosen, commanding the wide plain before it; and the central height was covered with batteries.

After passing a branch of the Ebro, we took post under cover of a hill, and waited further orders. Wellington, in the meantime, was massing troops on our right and left for a grand attack: and in him we had confidence.

While under the hill, the enemy dropped shells very plentifully over it, killing and wounding several. A corporal, six feet three inches high, was struck on the breast and killed by the splinter of a shell while holding the Colonel's horse.

A violent attack was first made by our men on the enemy's left flank, which was posted on a craggy height. The contest was long and severe; but at length they were driven from the hill. Their left being now turned and rolled up, a general advance was made. We marched across a flat covered with our splendid cavalry into a wood of fir trees.

Now the great tug of battle became fiercer, and the cannonading was tremendous and continuous, so that the musketry, which was also incessant, was lost in the horrid din caused by perhaps 200 pieces of artillery. The smoke, the hissing of balls and shells, and the rush of cavalry and flying artillery, with occasional hurrahs, formed an indescribable uproar. We debouched from the wood, and formed line in front of the light brigade, among whom I saw my brother, about fifty yards behind me. We nodded; and while doing so, a ball ploughed up the earth before him. On my right a ball tore a man's knapsack from his back, but did not kill him. Through a fine field of ripe wheat we advanced in line covered by a squadron of the Life Guards, and began to surround the French centre. Here the smoke was so dense that we could hardly distinguish friends from foes. After passing a fence, an officer galloped past our company and shouted, "We have taken forty pieces of artillery down there". This quickened our steps and pulses. A minute or two pass and Wellington with his staff gallops to a hill in our front and orders up six pieces of artillery, which instantly began blazing away at the enemy who were now in full and hasty retreat, Wellington in the mean time glassing the total route of the foe with great earnestness.

The uproar of battle now ceased as by magic, for the left wing of the army, perhaps two miles distant, had driven in the enemy's right upon their centre, and taken possession of the great high road leading to France. In consequence, the enemy beaten at all points, made a general rush for the road to Pampeluna, leaving behind them 151 pieces of cannon, 415 waggons laden with money, and provisions, etc., etc., besides all their cattle, sheep, and goats. Numerous carriages belonging to ladies and gentlemen, who had come from France to see the English beaten, blocked up the road. It was altogether a strange scene.

While marching rapidly in pursuit, our men began to load themselves with provisions which they seized in passing the deserted waggons. I picked up a whole sheep newly skinned, and my comrade shouldered the prize. While thus engaged, a general rode up, "Throw away your stuff, men, you will get plenty more just now." Down went the sheep, etc., and "Double quick, forward" off we went with some cavalry before us at a dashing pace over a plank bridge after King Joseph, who was not far in front. But Joseph saw his danger, sprang from his carriage, mounted a horse, and gave us the slip.

Pressing forward amidst the wreck of the enemy's stores, I came upon a sack of meal or flour lying on the road. Out of this I filled my haversack, and ran on with my scarlet jacket well powdered. Further on a bag of leaf tobacco came in my way. Of this, I tied up about two pounds in my sash. On, on we swept, and took possession of some hundreds of bullocks and sheep which the enemy had abandoned, after hamstringing some of the poor animals.

We halted at a beautiful village, and drove a lot of sheep and goats into an enclosure. Of these I had to take charge all night.

Now all set to work with coats off and sleeves up: the furniture of the house we occupied was smashed, and fires were lighted both inside and out of doors. Some killed sheep, while others made fat dumplings. A party here was frying chops; another party there smoking tobacco: all happy as princes. At a distance, in a house, a selfish few, who had found or stolen a cask of rum, were drinking copiously. This speedily put them to sleep. Being orderly serjeant, I went not near them. But I was not idle: I killed three sheep as my share, and made and baked, or rather burnt, several loaves, after which I milked some goats and had a splendid supper.

In the course of the night the money waggons taken from the enemy were plundered of perhaps nearly seventeen millions of francs. One of my company got his pockets filled with doubloons and dollars. My comrade got a donkey, which we loaded next morning with cooked mutton and other eatables. The spoil taken in this battle was very great. The enemy brought 153 pieces of artillery into the field, but they only carried off two pieces from it, and one of these we afterwards found abandoned on the road to Pampeluna.

On the second day's march I had one or two applications from officers for some of my stock of bread, etc. On the third day we encamped within view of Pampeluna. Having piled arms near the 43rd regiment, my brother came and made a sad complaint of being famished. He said he and his comrades had been obliged to eat bean tops for three days. I was happy in being able to supply him with some badly baked cakes, some flour, and a little money.

Pampeluna is fortified, and obtains water by means of an aqueduct two or three miles in length. We marched past it to Tiebas on the 26th, and next day to Traffala, and halted at Aybar. On the last day's march I was ordered to stay behind at two cross roads, to show the rear columns the route our division had taken to the mountains. The day was dreadfully hot, and having to hurry forward to join my regiment, I was sadly fatigued and unwell, caused by something like sun stroke.

The French being driven into France, we counter-marched to Pampeluna to join in blockading it. On this day's march I was taken ill of fever. After staggering on a few miles, I was obliged to fall out of the column, and sit down in a wood. The adjutant with whom I was a favourite passed by and said, I might come on leisurely. A plentiful bleeding at the nose rather relieved me. After the division had passed I rose and managed to join my company. Much against my will I went to hospital, where I had dreadful pains in my head, back, and bowels. These were followed by ague every afternoon.

In a few days the Conde-de-Abisbal brought up a body of Spanish troops and relieved us from the blockade.

It being known by the French that the garrison in Pampeluna was in great want of provisions; vigorous efforts were made by them to collect a strong force to relieve it. This done, General Soult attacked Hill's division with great fury. Hill retreated, and our division was ordered up to support him. Accordingly, all that could walk were sent from the hospital, and though I was very weak, I had to join my company and march with it next morning into the mountains. In two days we reached a small village called Espanhel, situated in the beautiful valley of Roncesvalles. The houses here are remarkable for size, and the valley for plenty of corn and grapes.

On the 24th, we climbed to the top of a high ridge in the middle of the Pyrenean range. I found this hard work, for some times I had, like others, to drag myself forward by the roots of trees: at other times I crept on hands and knees. However the fresh air did me good.

Battles of the Pyrenees

As the French in great force were now advancing rapidly upon us, we were kept marching and countermarching from ridge to valley, and from valley to ridge again.

In the afternoon, a detachment of the 20th regiment was sent up a mountain side to feel for the enemy. A dense cloud was hugging its summit and hiding the French. The detachment had hardly disappeared in the mist before they were attacked by overwhelming numbers. We heard a heavy roll of musketry, and in a few minutes saw our men retiring hastily before perhaps 2,000 of the enemy. We immediately moved up to their support, and skirmished in a wood till long after dark. When the firing had ceased, the sounds of suffering grated painfully on our ears. A few yards off, a wounded or dying Frenchman was crying out most piteously, "*Ah mon Dieu! Ah mon Dieu!*" ("O my God!") Close to my feet lay two of our men. One was dead, the other dying. The brains of the latter were protruding above his eyes. I knew him and thought he looked up to me; but there was no utterance or sound, sobs excepted.

The order to retire came along the chain of skirmishers in a whisper. While making this movement we came to an open space in a wood, where a number of our badly wounded were lying wrapped in their blankets.

They heard the rustle of our feet, and one of them asked, "What regiment is that?"

Answer "The seventh."

"Where are you going?"

"We are retreating."

"Will you leave us here?"

We stole away, and left them to the mercy of the enemy and the mountain wolves, not being able to take them off. We got no bread this day, and our rum was purposely spilled to prevent drunkenness. This night march was horrible, for our path lay among rocks and bushes, and was so narrow that only one man could pass at a time; consequently our progress was exceedingly tedious, stopping as we did five or ten minutes every two or three yards. This was made much worse by the pitchy darkness. Many were swearing, grumbling, stumbling, and tumbling. No wonder, we were worn out with fatigue, and ravenous with hunger. However I kept up, though my gaiter straps and one of my shoe ties were broken. I called the roll of the company when we halted, and was surprised to find every man present.

About noon next day we were favoured with some biscuit, and were preparing to cook when the enemy debouched from a wood in front, and began to drive in our piquets. Of course the cooking was stopped, and we retired to a new position. The retreating and cannonading continued till sunset, and then we cooked.

Large fires were lighted along the whole front at midnight, and then we retreated in almost impassible roads, till late next morning. We then took up position within sight of Pampeluna. Having now reached the limits of our retreat, we saw the different divisions converging, and unmistakable tokens of a crash.

To gain our position we had to climb a high ridge,

whose summit was not above a yard across. Its sides were so steep and slippery that we could hardly keep footing. Again our camp kettle was prevented from boiling by the command—"Fall in." My messmate and I carried the kettle down the slope and to the top of a still higher mountain, where a contest had been raging for some time between the French and two regiments of Spaniards, supported by our 40th. The enemy was driven back before we arrived at the top; but skirmishing was kept up below us till dark. While the firing continued, an elemental war was gathering above our heads. This soon burst upon us with terrible fury. The thunder and lightning were appalling, and the rain came down like a cataract. Though there was no shelter, the order was "No great coats or blankets to be loosed;" consequently we were miserably wet and cold, and passed a sad night among the grass. The storm quieted the fighting parties, and prevented our cooking.

Battle of Pampeluna

July 28th and 30th, 1813

Early in the morning of July 28th, we were under arms. The French covered the opposite heights, waiting orders to rush through the opening on our left. First, they sent forward a few cavalry with a trumpeter, along the opposite mountain, side to reconnoitre. We watched their progress till they came to a corner of the road, when suddenly they came scampering back. A few minutes afterwards a column of the enemy moved down on our left along the high road to Pampeluna. To prevent their passing we descended, and attacked them in flank. At the same time other heavy bodies were launched against our right and centre, and the firing became heavier and closer. The leading column of the enemy succeeded in passing us, and marched boldly forward to the brow of a hill 300 yards beyond our flank, when, to their surprise, a concealed division of ours rose up, and rushing upon them, poured a storm of fire into the loose mass which sent them back in disorder. Our fire was now redoubled, and was no doubt destructive. A Portuguese company of cassadores that was joined to us hearing the French crying out "*Espanhola! Espanhola!* "to make us believe they were friends, cried out "*No Espanhola! Maisfuego! maisfuego!* "("More fire! more fire!") We all did so, and men fell fast on both sides. While I was kneeling and firing, a drill-serjeant named Brooks, who afterwards got a commission, came and helped to get my cartridges out more quickly. We got on bravely until a ball knocked off his cap. He, perhaps thinking the place too hot, left me to help myself.

All our officers were at this time wounded. I helped one of them whose leg was broken out of the fray a few yards. A brother serjeant, a morose fellow, and no friend of mine, I helped upon the adjutant's horse. He was shot in the loins or spine. I think he died. Why he was my enemy I never knew.

In the midst of all this, was very ill; the fever and ague had returned most furiously. Parched with thirst, and pained all over, I could hardly drag my limbs along.

Major Crowder, who commanded the left wing of our regiment, now came, and seeing that our officers were *hors-de-combat,* ordered me to go and tell the colonel our case. In doing this, I had to pass through a cross fire. I found the colonel on foot close to the enemy. While speaking to him, the senior major's horse was killed close by the colonel, and some men were wounded just behind me. Without giving any answer to my request for officers, the colonel (Edward Blakeney) put his hands on my shoulders and said, "Serjeant Cooper, go up the hill and tell the bri-gade-major to send down ammunition immediately, or we must retire." This was necessary, as our men were taking cartridges out of the wounded men's pouches.

I scrambled up the steep, and performed my duty with difficulty, as my legs would hardly obey me. I then dragged a Spaniard with his mule laden with ball car-tridge down to my company. The poor fellow was terri-bly frightened at the whizzing of the balls about him, and kept exclaiming *"Jesous, Marea! Jesous, Marea!"* However, I pushed him forward to my former station. Having un-laden his beast, he disappeared in an instant.

Throwing off my knapsack, I smashed the casks, and served out the cartridges as fast as possible, while my comrades blazed away. Close by me, a serjeant named Tom Simpson sat, pale as death, on his pack, holding his breast. "Tom," said I, "are you wounded?" Tom spoke not. He had just received a shot in his left side.

Hardly had I served out the ammunition and thrown on my knapsack, before a swarm of the enemy suddenly rushed over the brow of the hill, and swept our much reduced company down the craggy steep behind. Some of them seized the captain of the 9th company, and attempted to pull of his epaulets, but he resented this by a blow of his left fist. However, he was led off a prisoner.

By jumping down among the rocks my dress cap fell off, having my forage cap in it, and thus I was left bareheaded under a blazing sun. However, whatever number of balls followed me, they all missed, and I had the pleasure of seeing a fresh body of red jackets coming in haste to our relief; and by them the enemy were swept off the hill in their turn.

With great difficulty I gained the hill top, and found the company and the rest of the regiment. After repeated attacks, and as many repulses, the enemy gave up the contest, and retired up the slopes.

On calling the roll I found my company had lost twenty men. One of these, named Malony, that I had returned as missing, soon after made his appearance. I said, "Malony, where have you been?"

"Fighting, sure," said Pat.

"You have been skulking." "Have I! Look there!" said he, ripping open his jacket and shewing his blackened breast. A ball had struck his breast plate. I could say no more; but I felt sorry for being so hasty. Our regimental loss this day was about 200.

During the night there was a panic: all started up in

an instant and seized their arms; but no enemy appeared. What caused the stir no one knew; but these panics frequently occurred.

Little was done on the 29th besides burying the dead; but on the 30th the game of war began again by our cannonading the masses that attempted to break through our line in two places. Both these attacks failed, and we had the pleasure of seeing them driven down the steeps in glorious confusion by our brave Light Division. Immediately after this repulse, of which we were only spectators, Lord Wellington ordered a general advance on the enemy's position, as they were observed retreating hastily towards France, and leaving the garrison of Pampeluna to its fate. That place soon after surrendered. Unfortunately, I was not able to move, being in a hot fit of ague. The doctor came to me as I was lying on the ground shaded by a bush and blanket.

"What ails you, Serjeant Cooper?"

"It's my old complaint, sir."

"Well," said he, pointing to the retiring columns of the enemy, "the French are off yonder; we cannot leave any one with you. When the fit goes off, go down to that village below, and report yourself to the first doctor you see."

Thus I was left alone on a mountain in a blazing sun, without water.

When a little recovered, I slung my knapsack and fusee, and tottered down the steep to the village of Scrauson, and threw myself down in a stable among some straw. Looking about, I saw a surgeon that formerly belonged our regiment. I told him my case and was directed to go to a large house close by and take charge of a captain and a lieutenant who were both mortally wounded.

"They are your own officers, and both will die," said he. "See that their servants do not rob them."

I went accordingly The captain was wounded in the left side, and go was the lieutenant, but the shot had gone quite through the lieutenant's body.

Lieutenant Frazer died on the second or third day after the battle; Captain Wemyss on the fourth or fifth. There was something very affecting in the case of the captain's death. He had a brother who was an aid-de-camp in General Hill's division, and who had been wounded some days before in a skirmish. He hearing that his brother was mortally wounded, rode off in search of him; but for some days fruitlessly. At last he ascertained where his brother was lying, and hastened to the place. A short time before he came to the door, the dying captain asked his servant if he could read. He said he could. "Then," said the captain, "take that Prayer Book, and read to me." The servant did so. Soon after, there was a loud knocking at the street door, and then a well known voice in the stairs. The dying man sprang from his bed, flew to the door, and fell dead into his brother's arms. His parents lived on Southsea Common in 1815, to whom I took a letter from our colonel, but did not make myself known. A coffin was made of some old furniture, and the captain was buried in a garden beside the lieutenant.

While here, I heard that one of my oldest comrades was lying wounded in the next house. Soon as possible I set off to see him, carrying some tea, etc. I found him in a large room that was full of wounded—all bad cases. His thigh was broken near the hip. I saw that my attention, and his own condition, affected him. I think there was a starting tear in the poor fellow's eyes. He might probably recollect his bad behaviour to me on two occasions. His wound proved mortal. Next to him, sitting on his bed, was a comrade Serjeant named Bishop, sadly disfigured with blood and bandages. A ball had passed quite through his head. I did not know him at the first look; but he knew me and moved. Whether he lived or died I never ascertained. In Clonmel, Serjeant Bishop married a young Irishwoman, who had just before been married to a drummer belonging to a regiment ordered on foreign service. She accompanied Bishop for three or four years in the Peninsula. Being one day caught stealing, the provost-marshal flogged her on the breech. After this she left poor Bishop, and went to live with Colonel E., of the —— regiment. In a corner close by lay a man that I knew very well, breathing hard, and quite insensible. He died, and was buried. But where? In a horse-dunghill!

Here for several days I had an ague fit every afternoon. While in one, Major Crowder, who was wounded in the late battle, called to see the two officers that I had in charge. He gave me a few words also which were encouraging. However, thank God, by taking a few doses of Peruvian bark, I got rid of my disorder for a short time.

After the death of the two officers, I was ordered to take charge of twenty-five wounded Frenchmen, and take them to Vittoria. To guard them, I had one corporal and six privates. When mounted on mules, with heads, arms, or legs bandaged, etc., they presented a strange sight.

Having delivered up my charge, I joined the depot at Vittoria. But rest was not allowed to any who could walk; therefore so soon as an officer, two serjeants, including myself, and twenty or thirty men were selected from among the convalescents, we marched to join the army. Before we left Vittoria I went to see a Spanish play acted. I understood little of what was said, but I saw enough in the obscene gestures and dancing that disgusted me.

I also saw in a field close to the town the 151 pieces of artillery which we took in the battle. They were indeed splendid cannon. But I had not curiosity to go over the field again.

After five or six days uneasy marching, we arrived at Wellington's head quarters at Lasacca, a small village surrounded by lofty mountains. Now my plague, the ague, came on again. Here we could hourly hear the thunders of the siege of St. Sebastian. One assault had been made, but our men were driven back with great loss.

Not discouraged, though in the presence of a large French army under Soult, Wellington determined to make another grand effort. Accordingly, an order was given to every regiment in our division to send one serjeant, one corporal, and twenty privates, to assist in storming this strong place. I volunteered as soon as I heard the order read. An old corporal, John Styles by name, stammered out "A—a—a— an' I'll g—g—g—go too." In a few minutes ten serjeants, and old Styles, volunteered as stormers. We assembled at the colours, and drew lots. The first serjeant who drew got the prize, went, and fell wounded. Old Styles also drew a prize; and when he came back to the tent, said in his way, "Now, my lads, I am going; and as I have heard of Heaven and Hell, lend me a coin, and I'll toss up and see which is my place if I fall." He did toss up; but I have forgot the result of the toss. Old Jack marched with the stormers next morning, and fell severely wounded by a musket ball through the knee joint in the breach. The struggle was very severe; but our troops succeeded. The town was taken. The old veteran was taken to hospital, and told that his leg must be amputated the next morning. But when the doctors came, Jack was drunk, and said that he and his leg should not be parted. The medical men left him, and his leg mended in a contracted state; and when strong he joined us in France. He was a cripple, but did his duty as before, and was present afterwards in the battles of Orthes and Thoulouse. Poor old Styles loved drink too well, and had at different times received about two thousand lashes.

General Soult knowing the famishing state of the garrison of St. Sebastian, pushed forward several thousand men over the Bidassoa river, which divides Spain from France. A Spanish column was sent down from the heights of St. Marcial to attack them, while we were kept on the hill in reserve, looking on. The Spaniards being under the command and eye of Wellington himself, drove back the enemy several times in gallant style, and finally over the river, which they did not again attempt to cross. We cheered the Spaniards heartily after each charge.

While the battle was going on in front between the Spaniards and French, a heavy cannonade on our left plainly told that our troops were storming St. Sebastian. Quite in keeping with this, a dense cloud enveloped us on the heights. The wind blew furiously; the rain poured incessantly. My case was such as I shall never forget. Wrapped up in a wet blanket, and shaking in the ague, I was nearly half dead in the morning.

However, when daylight appeared, we had the satisfaction of seeing Soult's legions in full retreat to France, climbing the steep sides of the mountain in front. To cheer us a little more, news arrived that St. Sebastian was taken. Next day we returned to our old quarters at Lasacco, and rested a few days.

When we got to our tents I was ordered on duty. Of course I dragged myself to the parade. The adjutant called me: "You have been ill a long time, Cooper, I'll give you an easier post. Go on the Provost Marshal's guard, and there you may get some rest." I thanked him, and went.

October 7th, some severe fighting took place; but we only acted as reserve. In all these conflicts the enemy were beaten. The last stand they made was on the slope of La Rhune, the highest mountain in that part of the Pyrenees. Its form is like the frustrum of a sugar loaf, about

7,000 feet high. The firing here continued till long after dark, and seemed to be in the clouds. From this point the enemy were soon dislodged, and we encamped on a height, whence we had a splendid view of France. The ridge on which we pitched our tents was not more than thirty yards across, and its sides were very steep, especially on the French side. In this high and exposed situation the wind sometimes blew down our tents. This was the case one dark wet night: while a storm was raging, the top of the tent pole burst through the rotton cap, and down came the dripping tent upon us, with all the firelocks, belts, pouches, caps, etc. in glorious confusion. Some laughed, but others did worse. It was no joke, however, for we were all naked.

October 31st, our regiment was sent to the top of the highest spur of La Rhune, and our company was ordered to descend the other side and reconnoitre. This movement drew out the whole French force in front of their numerous camps. We piled arms and walked about, while the French skirmishers below kept firing at us through a hedge. This was not pleasant, as we had no orders to return the compliment.

While this ugly fun was going on, a comrade serjeant and I laid down close together, as the weather was cold, and began talking, when suddenly my friend behind me cried out, "Oh! I've catched it." A ball had gone so far through his thigh, that it had raised up the flesh and skin on the upper side. Another pennyweight of powder would have driven it into my premises.

From the top of La Rhune a complete view of the redoubts and camps of the French could be obtained. A regiment of Spaniards occupied this elevated spot, and had to burrow like rabbits among the rocks. Report said that some of them were frozen to death.

To the eastward of our position the mountains had a splendid appearance: pile rose behind pile, till they were lost in the clouds. Many were covered with snow, which was in some places fourteen or fifteen feet deep.

In the valley behind our camp was a wood of chesnut trees. The fruit was plentiful, and when boiled made a good substitute for potatoes.

November 10th, an order came to move at a moment's warning; and at midnight we descended the heights in silence, and halted a little before daybreak near a redoubt occupied by the enemy. Just as day broke, the 2nd or Queen's regiment, with part of the 53rd, doffed their knapsacks, and dashed at the redoubt, surprised the sleeping garrison, and made them prisoners. Shots now began to be exchanged in rapid succession, and the battle began.

Battle of Vera

November 10th, 1813

Heavy firing on our left among the rocks above us, showed that the Light Division was hotly engaged. My brother, while running forward, was tripped up by a shot, which ripped off the sole of one of his shoes. Of course he went on without it.

The tide of war now rolled furiously onward; and the advance of our troops on the right, driving the enemy from hedge to hedge, and from wall to wall, was really brilliant.

If there was a stop for a moment or two, the next thing was a run and a cheer. At the same time the right and centre of the army moved on slowly, and threatened the enemy's rear. Near a gate way three or four fine fellows were lying dead belonging the 40th Light Company.

Pressing on, we came in front of a high conical hill, crowned with a strong redoubt, and defended by 900 Frenchmen. The firing was hot here, and the 52nd lost many at its base and sides. All cover on its slope had been removed. We halted on the left flank of this formidable redoubt, and expected an order to storm it. But at this moment Wellington and his staff arrived. An officer with a flag of truce was sent up to demand the surrender of the post.

I shall not forget the appearance of the officer who received the summons. He appeared like a madman; but seeing himself surrounded and cut off from the main body, he submitted. The garrison marched out, laid down their arms, and were marched off under an escort of Spaniards.

The enemy were now in full retreat from the sea on their right to their extreme left—a distance of perhaps five miles. All their numerous camps were in a blaze, the smoke of which obscured the whole country. By turning their left, and threatening to cut off their retreat to Bayonne, the batteries and breastworks which had cost them months of labour, were rendered useless. We encamped this evening on the banks of the Neville. After dark there was some firing between the piquets of both armies.

So ended the Battle of Vera, or the Forcing of the French 'Torres Vedras'.

November 11th, we marched to Le Boes-de St. Pe, and crossed the Neville. On the 17th we recrossed the Neville, and were quartered at Sarra. December 8th, again to St. Pe. Plenty of fruit. Very bad roads. Much rain and fog. On the 9th there was skirmishing in front of the intrenched camp near Bayonne. On the 10th we marched and took post near the church of Arcangues, and thence to Biaritz. Here the left wing of our army under General Hope was engaged with a strong force of the enemy; but they were repulsed with great slaughter. Previous to this attack a group of French officers ascended a small hill in our front. One, like the chief, dismounted, and placed his glass on his saddle. We said one to another, "That is Soult: now for a dust." So it happened; and the firing lasted till dark. Our company lined the hedges, but was not attacked.

About 10 p.m. two German regiments—*viz*: those of Nassau and Frankfort, left the French lines and came over to ours, with bugles sounding a quickstep. This caused a great sensation.

December 13th, we crossed the Nive to Villa Franca,

and thence to Ustaritz, where we slept in an open field without tents during a bleak frosty night. Next day we arrived at Arcangeu again, and began throwing up works near the church.

Here for the first time in the Peninsula we kept Christmas. Every man contributed some money, meat, or wine. A sheep or two were bought and killed. Pies and puddings were baked, etc. Plates, knives and forks, were not plentiful, yet we managed to diminish the stock of eatables in quick time. For desert we had plenty of apples; and for a finish, two or three bandsmen played merry times, while many warmed their toes by dancing jigs and reels.

Campaign of 1814

January 14th, we marched to Ustaritz. On the 6th there was a severe action in front of Bayonne; but it was over before we arrived, and the French were soundly thrashed by General Hill's troops, though the enemy were more numerous. After the action, the rain fell heavily, which chilled us to the bone, and put our fires out. This was one of our distressing nights. On the 7th, back to Ustaritz in horrible roads, cut up by artillery, cavalry, and donkeys. Shocking weather continued. Halted at Heneritz till February 16th.

On the 25th we crossed a branch of the river Adour, and slept in a low marshy field, after standing for hours in the rain.

On the following morning, cold as it was, we crossed another river. A soldier's wife, with two greyhounds in a string, slipt into deep water, and would have perished, had not the dogs saved her by swimming to the shore. After marching a few miles further, we crossed another river, which took the men up to their middles. Our company went down the bank and got over in a boat.

Having passed over a few fields, and gained the high road to Orthes, we moved forward through a thick wood, the right wing in front. On a sudden the words, "Open out right and left and let the artillery pass" were given. This we well knew was a sign the enemy was at hand.

Battle of Orthes

February 27th, 1814

It was surprising that General Soult did not try J to prevent our passage of the last mentioned river. Perhaps he wished us to get entangled among those streams, and then he would have a chance of giving us a thrashing; but Wellington was more cautious in all that he undertook than to risk the lives of his men without a prospect of victory.

The artillery having dashed past, our regiment was ordered to move to the left, in order to flank the enemy's right, and drive in the outposts. We directly surprised a piquet behind a farmhouse. They were busy cooking; but their bugler roused them, and they fell back firing briskly. In the flat below, the contest was sharp between the French skirmishers and ours. The main body of the enemy occupied a steep ridge with numerous artillery, which blazed away while we were massing and closing on them. Our company was posted behind a large building, and commenced firing in rapid bopeep fashion. Some of our men in the meantime broke into the house, and finding a store of wine, handed it out copiously to the combatants, so that the game was "Drink and fire, fire and drink." Others were engaged in stoning and bagging the wandering astonished poultry.

Tired of inaction, Serjeant Simpson, who was wounded, as before mentioned, on the heights of Pampeluna, shouted, "Come, let us charge these fellows!" Away he and most of the company went double quick, and drove the enemy from their hiding places: but poor Simpson received a shot which laid him dead. Receiving a reinforcement, the enemy drove our men back, and stripped our wounded of their knapsacks, etc. It was here that wicked man fell with both his legs broken who in my hearing several years before said, "I don't care a d—m for Jesus Christ." He died of his wounds at Orthes.

From behind the house I was sent with a party to make a circuit farther to the left, in search of French skirmishers that might be skulking behind hedges, etc. In our round we came to a deserted farm house. My companions would enter for plunder. I warned them of their danger, and moved on While they were rummaging the house, Lord Wellington and his Staff passed; but he being occupied with things of greater moment, did not notice us. We joined our company where two roads met, and had hardly taken breath before some of the enemy rushed up one of the lanes and opened fire upon us. Our captain turning round said sharply, "Give those rascals a charge." In an instant a few of us jumped over a hedge and at them. But they cut like rabbits, and we after them headlong. During the chase my bayonet flew off. I stopped not to pick it up, but plunged into a wood, firing as fast as I could, till my trigger finger was swollen as to be nearly useless.

Again and again the enemy rallied; but were as often repulsed. Now a pause ensued, which generally indicated a coming storm. Presently on came a long line of red jackets at quick step, a little to our right, and when within eighty or a hundred yards of the enemy, poured a terrible and prolonged fire upon them. This was answered by the French until the combatants were completely enshrouded in smoke.

The scattering of the powder cloud shewed the British closing on the foe; but they avoided the shock by going to the right about in great haste.

The right wing of our army was equally successful; and the enemy hurried from the field in order to gain the great high road. Our cavalry pursued them hotly for several miles, so that many of the enemy in their hurry threw away their arms.

Though sadly fatigued with this day's work, we moved on to Sault-de-Navailles.

Marched next morning, and passed one of our poor fellows, who had stolen some flour, hanging on a tree.

March 2nd, we moved to Granada in very wet weather, and found the French had blown up the bridge. Halted several hours in a down pour of rain, and were afterwards encamped in a boggy field, because several men were drunk.

Here old Jack Styles, who was wounded at the storming of St. Sebastian, was so wet, cold, and done up that, though he dearly loved drink, he would not rise for it.

While standing on the road, a laughable incident, occurred. A married man of our company, whose wife had procured a large loaf and given it to him, was standing on the edge of a deep ditch: his feet slipped, and he fell backwards, nearly over head in the water.

March 8th, we marched to Monte Marsan. In the market place of that town there is a fountain which, from two spouts, sends forth hot and cold water. On the 9th we marched to Roquefort, in a heavy fall of snow. Since my late illness my blood had got into an impure state. Large blotches had broken out, especially on my arms and legs. Having no drawers, my rough trowsers annoyed me dreadfully. Slept at night in a wood, stiff and sore.

In this part of France every thing was very cheap. Good

bread three *sous* per pound. Wine seven *sous* per bottle, etc. Sometimes the French people where we were quartered would treat us with bread and wine. After several marchings and counter-marchings we arrived at St. Martins, two miles south of the city of Thoulouse. Here General Soult had fortified the heights which overlook the city with many batteries and redoubts, and seemed determined to make a stand. The deep rapid Garronne was between us and the town; and the bridge head was strongly fortified.

Between St. Martins and the city there is an extensive flat, laid out in gardens and vineyards. On this our piquets were stationed, opposite to those of the enemy; and on the high road leading to the city two English soldiers were placed facing two of their foes. The two nearest each other were cavalry; the two behind infantry. There they watched each others movements at about seventy or eighty yards apart. One day after relief time, the French vidette suddenly galloped up to the English horseman, and announced himself a deserter.

April 3rd. After dark we marched a few miles down the river side, and took up our night's lodging in a soft stubble field, while the rain poured down for several hours.

Next morning we marched down to the river, and crossed by a pontoon bridge which had been hastily constructed during the night. At the same time, small parties of the enemy appeared on the opposite bank, and fired a few shots; but over we went with band in front playing the *British Grenadiers*. We afterwards marched a few miles, and were quartered in a church.

April 8th, we supported an attack made by the 18th hussars on the enemy's cavalry. The hussars behaved well, and took some prisoners, several of whom were sadly slashed about the head. Took up quarters in the evening at St. Dennis.

During the night, two men of our piquet left their posts, and were detected searching for wine beyond our lines. Of course they were flogged severely, and had to fight next day with their knapsacks in hand.

Early on the 10th of April, (Easter Sunday, 1814,) we formed close column at the bridge of Croix-de-Orade, and prepared to storm the intrenched heights.

Battle of Thoulouse

April 10th, 1814

When all was ready, we crossed the bridge, and marched about a mile along the bank of the river Ers, while the enemy poured their shot through our ranks. A man just before me had his firelock knocked off his left shoulder. During this movement the enemy had the game all to themselves, as they had blown up the other two bridges to prevent our passing in force.

Some time therefore was lost before our guns and cavalry came up, and before we arrived at the post assigned to our division, a large body of dragoons posted on the high road between two hills, seemed inclined to make a dash at us; but the rocket brigade joining us at the time they were about to charge, stopped them. The first rocket fired, went right into their column, and sent them scampering back.

Looking round, I was glad to see that our dragoons, having passed the narrow bridge of Croix-de-Orade, were coming up at a gallop. A column of Spanish infantry was now ordered to attack a strong redoubt on a height opposite the above mentioned bridge; but they were driven down again with great loss. Our Light Division, always ready, then formed, advanced, and settled the matter in a few minutes.

Having reached our post on the extreme left of the line,

we faced to the right, and advanced up the slope towards the batteries with bold front and bugles sounding.

The troops that were the nearest to the French batteries now closed upon the masses that came pouring over the hill, and the struggle became tremendous; but, as usual, the red jackets prevailed, and in a quarter of an hour we stood triumphant on the hill. Here we were ordered to lay down to avoid as much as possible a flanking fire that was kept up by the enemy.

A poor fellow that I had been talking to at the bridge was now borne along, his leg hanging by a bit of flesh. His wife was killed at Salamanca, while giving drink to a wounded man.

While lying on the ground, a round shot came bounding, and struck my mess tin, which was strapped on the top of my knapsack, and made a disagreeable ting. A serjeant lying close by exclaimed, "Jack! very near that time!" So I thought; and moved a little. This was closely followed by a musket ball whizzing past my head.

Having had several of my accoutrements stolen, I went among the dead to select such as I wanted. One of the 42nd, or Highland Watch, had a belt that suited me. Though he was not quite dead I stripped him of it. I also wanted a bayonet, therefore I went in search of one nearer the enemy's skirmishers, who were concealed under the brow of the hill; but the balls came too thickly to invite my stay there. Having got what I sought, I looked behind me, and saw Lord Wellington and his Staff riding along the ridge. I knew then the game the enemy aimed at. He took no notice of the *whiz*, *whiz*, but rode on.

Just after we gained the hill, a shell burst a yard or two before a loaded donkey driven by a soldier's wife, without doing either any harm. The woman was there contrary to orders.

Before 1 p.m. the enemy were beaten at all points, notwithstanding their superiority in artillery, cavalry, and fortified position; and it must have been extremely mortifying to them to be thus routed in the vicinity of one of their chief cities.

After resting a while, we advanced over the hill, and had a full view of the city into which the enemy were retreating. Halting on the slope in a column at quarter distance, the sound of approaching cavalry was heard on our flank. "Form square!" was the word. 'Twas done in an instant. The enemy saw this, wheeled about, and cantered down the hill. So ended the sanguinary Battle of Thoulouse, and our Easter Sunday services.

We fully expected the fight would be renewed next morning, as General Soult had said he would bury his army in the ruins of the city. But no conflict took place. As the ammunition of our artillery was nearly expended, men were sent to gather cannon balls off the field. Happily, there was no more occasion for them; for Peace had been concluded some days before. It was said, that the French General knew this before the battle. However, he and his beaten troops, evacuated the city next morning, and from our elevated position, we had a view of our retiring foes—foes no longer. On the 12th, we took possession of this old city, and then pursued the enemy to St. Felix. Being encamped on a hill, a hurricane arose which tore nearly all our tents to pieces, here the news of Peace arrived.

April 20th, we turned our faces homeward and marched through the streets of Thoulouse. There are some grand buildings in this city, particularly a large church or cathedral, and the town hall. This city I think is mentioned in Caesar's Commentaries. It is nearly 400 miles from Paris.

Continuing our march we arrived at the town of Condom, where we remained six weeks, among people well disposed towards the English.

Here I had to go to hospital for three weeks. I believe this place was a nunnery. Veiled ladies often passed through the wards, and seemed compassionate. In connection with the building, was a spacious square, in which our brigade assembled for divine service on Sundays, many of the inhabitants attending as spectators.

When the days were fine, a number of babies was brought out and placed in the shade of some spreading trees, in the square. These children might be foundlings, or perhaps, the friars could have told whose they were.

Having again recovered and joined my company, we inarched past the city of Bourdeaux, which is the finest town that I saw in France. Thence we moved to Sousam. This part of the country is extremely flat, without any fences, and thousands of sheep are tended upon it. The shepherds stalk about on stilts of ten or twelve feet high, bearing long poles in their hands. These men walking about in a foggy morning, present a strange appearance.

June 13th, we embarked at Poliac, near the mouth of the river Grarrone, on board the *Anderson* transport, and ran down to Verdum roads. From this vessel we were transferred to the *Clarence,* of seventy four guns.

Here the whole regiment, officers, men, women, children, and baggage were bundled and packed for England. One of the decks was cleared of guns, for our special use and comfort. Our regiment then numbered about six hundred: these with the crew, crowded the vessel. The sailors had hammocks, but we had only the deck, therefore at night we lay like a flock of sheep on a common. Consequently, when the ship rolled, as every one knows ships do, in the Bay of Biscay, there was sad squeezing as the vessel rocked from starboard to larboard, and vice versa. What made matters worse, the wind was foul and the ship close-hauled till we made the Eddystone lighthouse, near Plymouth.

June 27th, we anchored in Plymouth Sound. Soon after an order being given, over-board went all our blankets, jackets, and trowsers, with their numerous population. We disembarked next day, and marched to Portsmouth, where we arrived on the 18th of July, 1814, and were quartered in Colehouse Barracks.

Here we received our arrears of pay, of which some men had considerable sums due. But all soon went into the hands of landlords. The men were quite crazy until the money was spent. However, one meal a day soon sobered them. The period of my service, *viz.*, seven years, being within three weeks of its termination, I looked for my liberation every day. According to my wishes, the order to discharge all the seven years men arrived, and the documents were written forthwith.

But before the order was carried into execution, another came for our regiment to embark immediately on a secret expedition. Accordingly, we were hurried on board a transport, and sailed to Plymouth 5th October, 1814.

On entering the boat at Portsmouth, I gave an old comrade half-a-crown to buy me some bread, etc., but the rascal never came back.

We anchored in the Sound almost alongside the *Chesapeak* frigate which had been taken some time before from the Americans by the *Shannon* frigate.

The wind not being fair we remained at anchor till the 25th of October.

The clerks having made out our discharges, nothing was wanted to set us free but the Colonel's signature. Unfortunately, he was ashore. We were all on tiptoe to start for home, when we saw boat-loads of discharged men, belonging to the 43rd regiment, leaving the ships near us, and going on shore.

In one of them was my brother, with his discharge in his pocket. He came alongside, and called out, "Come, are you ready for Barnard Castle?"

I replied, " I only want my paper, but the Colonel is on shore. As soon as I get it, I will join you."

"Well," said he, "I will wait for you."

The boat then proceeded towards Plymouth.

In a few minutes after, the wind, which had been unfavourable for a fortnight, changed. Up went a blue Peter, as the sailors call it, to the mast head of our convoy, the *Venjeur,* a seventy-four, as a signal for immediate putting to sea. Anchor up, and away we sailed along the coast of Cornwall. I hoped that Cork would be our destination, but when off the Lizard, I found our course was much too southerly for that.

Next morning, I looked at the compass, and saw that our course was South by West. I did not fancy that. I had hoped that if the fleet put into Cork, we should get our discharges there.

In the very worst humour, we sailed past Gibraltar and Madeira. Between these two places, a heavy gale gave us a good taste of sea sickness. Perhaps a word or two respecting what those experience "who go down to the sea in ships, and do business in great waters," may not be out of place here.

When passing through the Bay of Biscay in 1809, the wind blew roughly, and raised a heavy sea in that notorious part of the ocean. Never having seen the sea in such mighty commotion before, I was frequently afraid when the vessel sank into a deep trough between towering mountainous waves, that we should be engulfed and go to the bottom; and when she rose to the crest of one of them our next plunge would be the last. I have passed through the Bay four times, but never saw it so rough as at our first crossing.

But it is in mid-ocean that the scene in a storm is on a grander scale. To windward rises a mountainous ridge of water, and comes onward, threatening to bury in its bosom all that comes in its way. The wind and sea join in one mighty roar. The ship is struck by gigantic waves again and again with terrific force, and heeled half over. The wind whistles horribly in the rigging; the masts creak and bend; the ship groans under the terrible pressure as in an agony. Sometimes a mighty wave strikes her side or bows, mounts over her bulwarks, and rushes along the deck, carrying away every loose thing from stem to stern.

In the vicinity of the tropic of Cancer, we saw many strange fish, such as dolphins, flying fish, porpoises, etc., etc. One of the sailors struck a dolphin with a harpoon, but it immediately gave itself a jerk, broke the shaft of the implement, and cut with half of it sticking in its back. A huge grampus also gambolled round the vessel.

November 17th, we crossed the tropic, and witnessed the strange ceremony of ducking, etc. An old seaman dressed in a whimsical manner, standing on the bow of the ship, bawled through a speaking trumpet, "What ship is that? Whither are you bound? Have you any on board who have not been in my dominions before?" etc. The captain replied to each question most submissively, saying he had several such persons on board, real green horns. Neptune, personated by the old seaman, then came into the forecastle, was seated on a gun carriage, to which ropes being attached, he was dragged along the gangway to the quarter deck, the captain saluting his grim majesty. The long boat had been previously filled with salt water for the ducking. A bucket, and an iron hoop, instead of a razor, were also in readiness for the shaving. The bucket, or lather box, was half filled with a compound of tar, grease, and something I shall not name. The razor was about a yard long, rusty and jagged at its edges.

Then a seaman, who was not willing to pay the usual fine, *viz.*—half a gallon of rum, was seated on the thwarts of the boat and blindfolded. An old tar then proceeded to lather the poor fellow most outrageously, at the same time asking sundry questions, in order that he might have an opportunity of thrusting his brush into the patient's mouth. Having satisfied himself with lathering or daubing the sufferer, the barber began with the hoop to scrape off the lather and a little skin from the man's jaws.

This savage operation was finished by the barber pushing his patient backwards overhead in the boat. The soldiers looked on, but would not stand shaving. The sailors, however, ascended the rigging, and threw buckets of water upon the red jackets. To prevent quarrelling, which was beginning, orders were given that the dashing and splashing should cease. Notwithstanding, some blows were exchanged.

During our voyage we had to parade on deck in heavy marching order every Sunday morning. This was annoying in a small ship. After we crossed the tropic, every man was frequently required to drink a pint of salt water on parade. One man, an old soldier named William Crumpton, said he could not swallow it. He did not drink any, and for this disobedience he received 150 lashes.

December 4th, we made the towering island of Dominica, and sailed through the channel which separates it from Martinique.

On the 9th we passed the island of St. Domingo. Being becalmed, soundings were taken, and the depth found was 184 fathoms. Some of the transports, attempting to go ahead of our convoy, were fired at with ball.

On the 10th we lay too off Port Royal, the capital of Jamaica, until the *Statira* frigate joined the fleet. She had Sir Edward Pakenham, the Commander-in-Chief of our expedition, on board. This vessel was soon after wrecked between Cuba and Jamaica. We passed Cape St. Antonia, the westermost point of the island of Cuba. After this we had a stiff breeze from the N. W. accompanied with heavy fog. Being on deck between six and seven a.m., I counted sixteen or seventeen water spouts a few miles off.

On the 31st we made the mouth of the Missisippi. The land here is very low, and the sea not more than four fathoms.

Campaign of 1815

The fog still continuing, we cruized for several days in search of the fleet. At last we discovered it, near Cat Island, where we anchored. Several regiments had landed, and been engaged in the night time with the Americans. They stole upon the English on their hands and knees, in Indian fashion, and penetrated the very camp; but they were driven out in quick time. This encounter took place several days before we arrived.

The day after we joined the fleet we were conveyed in small craft to the main land. One of our boats, containing sixteen privates and a serjeant, was swamped, and all but one were drowned.

After landing, we marched towards New Orleans, each man carrying a cannon ball in his haversack, as we had no baggage animals. Now two balls would have been more easily carried than one, because they would have poised each other.

'Tis said "delays are dangerous." So we proved it. The troops that had preceded us had been on shore about three weeks; but not being strong enough to meet the enemy, they had not advanced far from the sea.

As the fleet could not approach within about forty miles of the position, all the artillery, ammunition, and provisions, etc., had to be brought to us in boats. While all went on so tardily, the Americans were cutting trenches, mounting cannon, etc., across a narrow plain, which had the mighty Missisippi on the right, and a marshy dense wood on the left. A frigate also was posted on the river in such a situation that it could rake the whole line. Batteries were also planted on the right or farther bank of the river.

The force which the Americans had to defend this narrow front was said to be about 14,000. A deep wide ditch, in front of high breastworks, ran along the whole line of defence. Our whole force for attacking this formidable work, did not exceed 7,000, including several hundred sailors sent from the fleet.

The front of our position was perfectly flat, on which three small guns were planted; but these were of little use, being only six pounders.

On the day before the battle, I, with three or four more, was selected to join my old comrades in the light company, from which I had been transferred when made serjeant; but the captain would not let me go back. This probably saved my life, for the light company, with a company of the 43rd, and one of the 85th, stormed the right redoubt next day, and would have established themselves there had they been supported.

The same evening, hearing that we were to storm the enemy's works in the morning, several of us went to the colonel's tent, and reminded him that we should have been discharged at Portsmouth, and sent home, according to orders from the Duke of York, then Commander-in-Chief. He said it could not be helped. This did not satisfy us, so we hurried to head quarters, to speak to Sir Edward Pakenham, but he was out viewing the enemy's defences.

Battle of New Orleans

January 8th, 1815

Early in the morning of January 8th, 1815, we were assembled within cannon shot of the American entrenchments, as the reserve or second line. This was certainly a grand mistake, for the troops in front were composed of two black West India regiments, and other corps that had not been employed in sieges, etc., as we had in Spain.

Just as the day was breaking, a rocket whizzed aloft. All stood ready for the assault. At the word "Forward!" the two lines approached the ditch under a murderous discharge of musketry; but crossing the ditch and scaling the parapet were found impossible without ladders. These had been prepared, but the regiment that should have carried them left them behind, and thereby caused, in a few minutes, a dreadful loss of men and officers; while the enemy suffered little, being ensconced behind the parapet. The front line now fell into great confusion, and retreated behind us, leaving numerous killed and wounded. We then advanced to within musket shot; but the balls flew so thickly that we were ordered to lay down to avoid the shower.

In the meantime our light company and the two companies before mentioned had gained a footing on the right of the American works; but having no support at hand, the enemy returned in force and drove them into the ditch, where they were exposed to a plunging fire from above, and a flank fire from the frigate. One of the officers in the ditch vented his spleen at the enemy above by throwing stones. At last, the companies bolted from the ditch, and ran off stoopingly in different directions. One of them, named Henry Axhorn, a smart young fellow, received a ball above his hip, which ran up his body, and stuck near his eye. It was extracted in a hospital at New Orleans. He joined us again after the peace, much altered in shape, and not fit for further service. Our light company went into this action sixty-four strong, and returned sixteen—having lost forty-eight.

That part of our force which was despatched to storm the enemy's works on the other side of the river, pushed off when the rocket was fired; but being few in number, they effected nothing of importance.

On our part, just before the order was given to lay down, my right hand man received a bullet in his forehead, and fell dead across my feet. This man was drunk the night before, and cursing the seven years' men for their wishing to be discharged. Poor Fitzpatrick had been considered an honest man; but his knapsack, when opened, showed him to have been a sly thief.

Another man, about ten or twelve files on my right, was smashed to pieces by a cannon ball. I felt something strike my cap; I took it off, and found a portion of his brains sticking to it, about the size of a marble. A young man on my left got a wound on the top of his head, and ran to the surgeon behind us: he was dressed and sent into his place again. Close to him, another man had his arm, near the shoulder, so badly fractured that it was taken out of the cup. A few yards behind sat a black man, with all the lower part of his face shot away; his eyes were gone, and the bones of his brow all jagged, and dripping blood.

Near him, in a ditch, lay one of the 43rd, trying to hold in his bowels.

The enemy kept pounding away at us all day; during which, a shower of grape came whizzing like a flock of partridges, and struck Major King dead.

We lay on the ground under the enemy's fire until dusk, when we retired four or five hundred yards, and took up our quarters in some huts made of sugar canes. Here, without a single breastwork, battery, or ditch, we remained ten days; while the enemy threw shot and shell into our lines day and night. However, they took care not to leave their works.

The day after the battle, a truce for six hours being agreed upon, a party of us was sent to bury the dead. In this sad duty, the Americans brought ours to a ditch between our lines and theirs, and laid the bodies in rows. We then took them and threw them into ditches. While this was being done, an American officer strutted about, sword in hand, on his side of the ditch, to our great amusement. An American soldier, looking at the long rows of the slain, exclaimed, "I never saw the like of that!" One of our party sneeringly said, "That's nout, man; if you'd been wi' us in Spain, you would ha' seen summat far war!"

While removing the bodies, I stript two poor fellows of their shirts; they were bloody enough, but I wanted them sadly.

The funeral being over, and the truce having expired, we retired to our huts in haste, and then the game of cannonading began again.

The Americans were highly elated at having beaten the Britishers, and I believe they boast of it to this day. But all things considered, they had little reason. Let us recapitulate—they were in number about 14,000, behind strong breast works, and a deep ditch; a frigate protected their right flank, a wood and morass their left. Cannon was plentiful all along their front.

Our force numbered about 7,000, including perhaps 1,000 sailors. We had no works, no ditch, and only three small guns. Shelter we had none, for the ground in front of the enemy's works for about a mile was as flat as a bowling green.

Of the 1,200 that should have crossed the river, no more than three or four hundred could be supplied with boats. But the chief cause of our failure was the want of ladders, which a certain regiment should have carried, but did not. Had Wellington been there, the Americans would have had less to boast of. Why did not the redoubtable General Jackson, when we were reduced one third, attack us? Nay, why did he not do so, when all but about 1,800 of us had embarked?

Exposed as we were to the enemy's fire, brushing and parading were continued. Getting myself ready for parade one morning, I saw a man who was doing the same, struck by a round shot. Another, lying in his hut, had both his legs shot off. One day I had occasion to fetch water from a ditch in front of our lines; seeing a smoke rise from the enemy's batteries, I perceived a ball coming straight at me. To avoid it, I fell flat. However, it struck in boggy ground just before me, and sank. A shell fell one night within three feet of the hut in which four of us slept: it burst, made a large hole, but did no harm. I never heard the explosion. Another of these ugly customers passed over us, and dropped upon a man's knapsack, and drove it several feet down in the soft earth.

Being on piquet one day about a quarter of a mile in front, we were alarmed by the rattling of musketry on our right. Not seeing any enemy, our officer asked three of us to go into the thick wood with him to reconnoitre. After wading half-leg deep in water among stumps and tangled fallen trees, we found it next to impossible to proceed, and therefore gave up the enterprise. Our piquet post was a narrow mound of earth, about twenty paces long by two and a half broad, with water on both sides. By continued tramping this wet spot became a puddle. No fire could be lighted, lest we should draw the enemy's shot upon us. Having no alternative, I broke small branches from the bushes, and lay down in the mire. My stockings and shoes being wet, sleep I could not for shivering. Several of our men deserted while we remained in our lines.

Our situation now grew more critical every day, for nearly all the troops encamped behind us had embarked: the 40th regiment and ours alone remained.

On the evening of the 18th, the order to retreat came, and we began to move after darkness set in, leaving the piquets at their respective posts. The road we took had never before been trodden by man, and it was both difficult and dangerous. To construct it, small parties had been employed in treading down the tall reeds or canes that grew on the edge of a deep creek. These being twelve or fourteen feet in length, when trodden down, overlapped each other, and so formed a kind of basket road. This strange path, being underlaid by a stratum of rotten bog, was deceitful; and the night being dark, no one could see where to step. One officer slipped through this bending, swinging path, and sank to his armpits. A canteen strap put under those parts served to hoist him out of his dilemma. A bugler of the 95th Rifles sank overhead and was lost. I had a taste of the same, but only with one leg; the other stood on firmer stuff.

We marched in this way till near daybreak, when we were completely stopped by a wide, deep bog, like a cesspool. Till the foremost got over, we lay down till daylight among the wet grass. In this horrible swamp three or four poor fellows were sticking up to their middles. They were still sinking, and would have perished, when a boat having Admirals Malcolm and Cockrane on board, came down the creek. The boat stopped, and some sailors with shovels cut the prisoners out.

I made a short circuit, and got safely over by stepping on the roots of some large plants that grew there. Just beyond the bog lay a splendid dead alligator, twelve or fourteen feet long. At length we reached the sea side, and encamped. Not a shot had been fired at our rearguard during the retreat.

About three days after this, we embarked on board the *Fox* frigate. Here several boats came alongside, full of women belonging to the 93rd regiment, seeking their husbands; but as that corps had lost five or six hundred men on the 8th, many of these poor creatures would seek in vain.

We sailed the same day, but the old *Fox* ran aground, and stuck fast on a sand bank. Leaving the planks of the *Fox,* we were conveyed in small craft to Dauphine Island.

In this short passage, a young Swedish sailor slipped over the bow of the vessel into the sea. We looked for him astern but he never rose.

Having landed, we constructed huts. This island is nothing more than a great sand bank about twenty miles long, by one and a half broad. There is only one house upon it, and perhaps the reason it is not more inhabited is its want of fresh water. We made holes in the sand, which soon filled; but the water was brackish.

From this place troops were sent to take Fort Boyer, near Mobile. This was soon done, and our men returned, bringing the starred and striped colours of the 2nd Yankee regiment.

Next day a frigate arrived with the news that peace had been concluded between England and the United States. Had the ship conveying this information arrived sooner, the battle of New Orleans would not have been fought. Hearing this, the surviving seven years men, including myself, became impatient to be sent home; instead of which, we were ordered to construct a theatre. One was presently built of the branches of trees; scenes and dresses were improvised, and plays were acted: both officers and men taking part.

On the north-west of this island there is a bed of monstrously large oysters. Some of our men got large quantities. I cannot say that I liked the appearance of them.

Great pools of brackish water, ten or twelve feet deep, were common in the central parts of the island, in which alligators were seen.

One night a soldier's wife had a narrow escape from the jaws of one of these animals that was seeking its supper. The hut in which she and her husband were sleeping, was near the edge of one of these tiny lakes, and being without a door, was very handy for a visitor. An alligator having a stomach complaint, crawled out of the water and put his head into the hut, ready to borrow either a leg or an arm. Feeling an unusual weight upon her knees, the woman screamed, and frightened the animal back into the water. This being reported in the morning, a party was sent to shoot the animal when it rose to breathe. So, whenever its muzzle appeared above water, it received a bullet about its eyes. At last, being mortally wounded, it crawled out and died. Its carcase afterwards graced the theatre, and the bows of the *Seahorse* frigate in her voyage home.

One day, a large snake rose out of the sand in our tent, and kicked up a dust among us; but his capers were soon ended.

At last the whole fleet arrived from New Orleans, and proceeded to get in wood; consequently we had plenty to do in cutting down trees and carrying them to the boats. We embarked on the 28th March, 1815, on board the *Diomede* of fifty guns, and sailed for England on the 5th of April, accompanied by the *Ceylon* transport, leaving the rest of the fleet at anchor. Calms detained us much till the 9th, when a fine breeze sprung up, and we entered the harbour of Havannah, the capital of the island of Cuba, on the 21st.

This city was once taken by the English; but the inhabitants say we could not take it now. I think quite differently. Here is plenty of cocoa nuts, yams, bananas, pineapples, oranges, lemons, bread, wine, etc., very cheap. We also got twenty bullocks, to supply us with fresh meat on our voyage home. These animals were placed in the forecastle, and were a real nuisance while they lived.

On the 24th we sailed, and crossed the tropic of Cancer the fourth time, and entered the Behama channel, or gulf stream, in company with the *Volcano* bomb ship. As the Behama islands are numerous and dangerous, a sharp look out was ordered; nor was this unnecessary, for about four a.m., April 31st, a blue light was thrown up by the *Volcano* bomb as a signal of danger. The lieutenant of the watch, alarmed by the sudden light, looked ahead, and perceived the land close on the starboard bow. In a few minutes we should have been ashore and probably wrecked. The seaman whose business was to look out for danger was on the starboard foretopsail yard arm. He was ordered down, and promised six dozen lashes for his neglect. After a good deal of bustling, the ship was brought round. Getting clear of the island, and having a fine quarter breeze, we sometimes made more than 200 miles in twenty-four hours, though the old *Diomede* required pumping every four hours.

May 5th, we had all the studsails set, and were careering over the waves in grand style, when suddenly the wind chopped about fifteen or sixteen points. By this change, the ship was fairly caught, and staggered like a drunken man, so that the seamen were afraid of her going down stern foremost. Providentially the larboard foretop studding sail boom broke short off and eased the vessel. There were also some more smashes aloft; but nothing further happened. On the 7th had pleasant weather, and ran eleven or twelve knots per hour, although the old crazy vessel leaked three or four feet every watch.

At daylight on Whitsunday morning we discovered a French ship with jury masts. We bore down alongside, and hailed, "What ship is that?"

"The —— from Rochelle!"

"What news have you?"

"Buonaparte has escaped from Elba, and got to Paris, where he has 200,000 men in arms!"

My stars, what a sensation!! The news flew like wild fire along the decks. "We're in for it again!" said some. Others said, "You seven years' men will not get off now."

A horrible bustle ensued. The cannon which had been sent below to make room for us were hoisted on deck, and made ready for action.

On entering the English Channel we had a gale, and ran twelve or thirteen knots with only a double reefed foresail. May 31st, we rounded the Isle of Wight, and anchored at Spithead.

No sooner had the telegraph indicated our arrival to the War Office, than an order was sent by the same medium, that we should sail immediately to Ostend, and join Wellington at Brussels. However, in the afternoon, all the seven years men were discharged: we got our papers and were free.

After all our services, we were not favoured with boats to take us ashore, therefore we hired them, and landed at Portsmouth.

Having received my arrears and other monies, I arrived at home on the 5th of June, 1815; a fortnight before the Battle of Waterloo. Our regiment sailed almost immediately after we left, but did not arrive in time to take part in that great and decisive conflict.

In 1818 I applied personally to Marshall Sir John Berresford, who was visiting at Rockeby Hall, respecting my obtaining a pension. His answer was, "The rules are now so stringent that no limited service man can claim a pension unless he has been wounded." I applied again in 1833, through Colonel George Macleod, and received a similar answer.

In 1865, just fifty years after being discharged, I tried a third time, and obtained one shilling per day. I also received from Lieutenant General Charles Fitzroy Somerset (Lord Raglan) a Medal with Nine Clasps, bearing the words:

TALAVERA, BUSACCO, ALBUHERA,
CUEDAD RODERIGO, BADAJOZ, VITTORIA,
PYRENEES, ORTHES, THOULOUSE.

On the other side of the Medal, and on a silver plate attached to it, I have had engraved all those inferior engagements, skirmishes, etc., at which I was present, *viz*:—

OPORTO, REDINHA, FUENTE GRINALDO,
ALDEA-DE PONTE, CAMPO MAYO,
OLI-VENZA, MONTE LETTE, RONCESVALLES,
SARRA, ST. MARCEAL, VERA, NEW ORLEANS

N.B. I may here remark that in all the above, with the exception of New Orleans, we were never defeated, nor did we ever lose a single piece of artillery.

List of the Killed and Wounded

...in the 7th Royal Fusiliers, during the six Peninsular Campaigns of 1809-1814, with those who died in Hospital of Wounds, Fevers, and other diseases—

	Killed	Wounded
Officers	22	53
Serjeants	11	64
Rank and File	253	1074
	286	**1191**
Died in Hospitals		1700
between		20

Construction of the Peninsular Army

The English Army in the Peninsula was divided into seven divisions of Infantry, called the 1st, 2nd, 3rd, etc., division. Each division consisted of three brigades, and each brigade of three regiments. When the Portuguese troops were joined to the English, a Portuguese brigade was placed in the centre of some divisions. To each division was attached a brigade of artillery, viz., five guns and one howitzer. Each division had its General-in-Chief; each brigade had also a General; and each regiment a Colonel or Commanding officer.

The cavalry were also divided into brigades, as the Hussar brigade, etc.

The Duke of Wellington was Commander-in-Chief, assisted by what is termed a Staff, *viz.*, an Adjutant General, a Quartermaster General, a Paymaster General, a Commissary General, a Postmaster General, etc., with Aides-de-Camp and Brigade Majors, etc., etc.

The duties of the Adjutant General were to receive returns of the state, number, etc., of each division daily, and to transmit them to the War Office; and also to distribute orders to the divisions.

The Quartermaster General pointed out the stations of divisions, brigades, regiments, etc., in camp or quarters.

The Paymaster General paid the troops when he could get the cash.

The Commissary General issued rations when they were to be had.

The Postmaster General transmitted such letters to England as he thought proper.

To each division was also attached a notable personage called Provost Marshal, whose business was to flog or shoot marauders, etc., when he could catch them.

MARCHING, &C.

When the army, or part of it, had to move, orders were conveyed to divisions, brigades, etc., by dragoons. Sometimes the orders were to march instanter.

In hot weather we generally marched an hour or two before daylight. A halt generally took place every three or four miles for about twenty minutes, in order that the rear might close up: but when the roads were very bad, the rear got little or no rest. To obviate this evil, the division or brigade marched right or left in front alternately.

The order of march was in sections of threes. In summer, the march of a brigade might be seen at a great distance, by the great cloud of dust which enveloped it. The suffering of the men in these dust clouds was dreadful, from the heat, thirst, heavy roads, tight clothing, cross belts, and choking leather stocks. When we came to cross a stream, no halt was allowed; therefore hands or caps were dipped in the water as we went over it. Any stop would have thrown the whole column into confusion.

In rainy weather, the muddy roads were rendered nearly impassable by the march of artillery, cavalry, infantry, baggage, etc.

ENCAMPING

During the years 1809-10-11 and 12 the Peninsular Army was without tents, except at the third Siege of Badajoz. This want of shelter cost hundreds of lives. Sleeping in the open air is termed bivouaing, and the places chosen for it are eminences, woods, or the sides of rivers. When a column approached the place chosen for encamping, the orderly serjeants were summoned by bugle to the front, to take up ground for their respective companies. An open column was then formed on the serjeants, the arms were piled, and the cross belts and caps hung upon them.

The next thing was hut building: then parties were sent off in search of wood and water. Sometimes those parties travelled two or three miles for these necessary articles, particularly in Spain.

Frequently after the men and officers were hutted and resting, the bugle has sounded, and we have marched some miles further; and then it was wooding, watering, and hutting again. Once in such a case we left some scores of our brigade bathing in a river: of course there was a great scramble to overtake us.

As the bivouacs were frequently in strange localities, we were often obliged to cut down trees and bushes, and remove stones—which proceeding did not suit the snakes, lizards, centipedes, and scorpions that were plentiful in those places.

During our long marches we became ragged, shirtless, stockingless, and shoeless. In 1809 all the stockings I had were in my shoes, and the sole of one of my shoes was many a mile behind me. I have known more than 100 of the men of our regiment without shoes at one time.

When tents were issued to us in May, 1813, at the rate of three tents to a company, a great change was felt in the way of comfort. The number in each tent was generally about twenty. When these were all laid, none could turn without general consent, and the word "turn" given.

It sometimes happened, when the weather was stormy, that the tent pegs gave way, or the tent pole broke or went through the top, and then the row and confusion were horrible.

In bivouacs, as in tented camps, cooking was performed in rear of the camp. Mounds of earth were thrown up, and square holes dug in their sides for the fires.

The encampments of the hostile armies, sometimes numbering together, as at Busacco, about 130,000 men, had an imposing effect after dark with their 10 or 15,000 watch fires.

EATING, &C.

When a man entered a soldier's life in 1806, he should have parted with half his stomach. Our rations in England and Ireland were a pound and a half of bread, three-quarters of a pound of beef, bone included, for twenty-four hours. The beef was always boiled, and yielded a pint of broth to each man. Picking of teeth was not at that time much practised, or wanted.

In the Peninsula we were allowed a pound and a half of soft bread, or one pound of biscuit; one pound of beef or mutton; one pint of wine, or one-third of a pint of rum: but no vegetables. Sometimes we were reduced to half rations, and once, for a whole week, we had nothing but one pound of bad beef daily. When bread could not be obtained, we got a pint of unground wheat, or a sheaf of wheat out of the fields, or else two pounds of potatoes. No breakfasts, no suppers, no coffee, no sugar, in those days.

Dress

The dress of a soldier at that time was not for use, but show, like a child's doll in a toyshop.

Take for example one of the 7th Fusiliers full dressed. On his head he wore a cap covered with heel-ball, polished like a mirror. On the cap, under a varnished rosette, stood a tuft of wool six inches long, neatly trimmed. This weighty cap, or rather helmet, had nothing attached to prevent its falling off. When it did, it took hours to repair the damage.

All his hair, except a little on the sides and front, was tightly bound round a piece of lead behind. The hair on the sides was rubbed round till matted, then greased and powdered with flour. The whiskers were greased, set up, and also powdered.

About his neck he wore a stock of stiff leather four inches broad, well varnished. This thing was a real nuisance.

Projecting two inches from his breast, he had a neatly crimped ruffle. On his shoulders there were two wings made of cloth and wool, neatly combed and trimmed. The wings were useful in keeping on the cross belts.

His jacket fitted far too tightly; his buttons were bright as silver; and the lace on his breast and cuffs were white as pipe clay could make them.

His breeches were of white cloth, and reached a little below the knee; his long gaiters were black, and both breeches and gaiters were tight of course.

To bring all parts of his dress and accoutrements into

close contact, there were loops, loops, loops; loops to the gaiters; braces to the breeches; loops to the jacket; loops to the cross belts; loops to the wings, etc., etc. Should he try to reach the ground, it would have been fatal to some article of his set-off. Nothing could be contrived worse for real service.

WORK

To be tolerably fit for parade required three hours' work. His pouch, magazine, and bayonet scabbard, were covered with heel-ball like his cap. The barrel of his musket; the outside and inside of the lock; the bayonet, and the ramrod, must be polished like a razor. In addition to the above, he had to clean white leather gloves, cap and breastplate; his great coat must be neatly rolled up, and be exactly eighteen inches long. When blankets were issued, they had to be folded to suit the square of the knapsack. Many other things required polishing besides those already mentioned, as the gun brasses, picker, and brush and bayonet tip, etc., etc.

With the soldier of to-day things are greatly altered. Heel-ball, bright arms, ruffled shirts, white breeches, long hair, grease, hair powder, varnish, spirit of wine, and long fasts, are done away. Flogging is also reduced to a minimum. War too is at a discount; so let it ever remain.

State of the Hospitals Where I Was

The Hospital at Olivenza was a long low room, with another at a right angle to it; crowded with fever patients; the ventilation bad; many deaths daily.

The Hospital at Villa Vicoisa was in a convent; about 150 patients in the four corridors; next to no ventilation; small windows; great barrels or tubs for all purposes; the stench horrible; logs of fir burning at the four corners of the building, to drive away the infection; smoke blinding.

The Hospital at Elvas—a long bomb proof room; no ventilation, except by the door and chimney; twenty patients, of whom eighteen died. Convalescent room at Elvas; pavement bed for 1,000 or 1,500 men.

The Hospital at Guarda—miserable like the above.

The Hospital at Celokica—two small rooms, crowded with sick; no ventilation; no chamber utensil; the patients nearly all delirious.

www.ingramcontent.com/pod-product-compliance
Lightning Source LLC
Chambersburg PA
CBHW020505100426
42813CB00030B/3130/J